Machine Knitting Techniques

Fair Isle

Nic Corrigan

Machine Knitting Techniques

Fair Isle

THE CROWOOD PRESS

CONTENTS

INTRODUCTION

WHAT IS FAIR ISLE KNITTING?

The knitting term Fair Isle has evolved from a tiny, remote Scottish island in the Shetland Isles called Fair Isle. The island became renowned for a specific type of patterned knitting that used multiple colours in combinations of repetitive traditional motifs to create pleasing symmetrical designs that became very fashionable from the early twentieth century. It was used on everything from jumpers and cardigans to hats, gloves, scarves and more.

It is similar in nature and style to many other traditional vernacular patterned knitting styles, such as Norwegian, but true Fair Isle had certain rules that were always followed, and often certain families would have their own unique designs and combinations that would be handed down through the generations.

Since then 'Fair Isle' has become a general term that is used widely in both hand and machine knitting. In its simplest terms it means knitting a pattern with more than one colour in the same row. Traditionally this should mean just two colours in the same row but over time this has deviated and is generally accepted to cover any number of colours knitted together. However, in the context of this book, and machine knitting specifically, Fair Isle definitely means only two colours in the same row. It is not physically possible to use any more colours than this without some hand manipulation or by using a different technique such as intarsia. More specifically, for machine knitting, the term Fair Isle refers to using the Fair Isle function on your machine carriage, and for this only two colours are ever possible.

Fair Isle knitting falls in and out of fashion over time but is currently having a resurgence; popular designers such as Mati Ventrillon and Marie Bruhat both still live and work on the tiny island. The growing popularity of Shetland Wool Week is a testament to the enduring appeal and people travel from all over the world every year to visit and learn from the true experts.

Machine knitting is mixed in with this history. Domestic knitting machines with punchcards and a Fair Isle function emerged in the late 1960s and this allowed the knitter to thread up two different colours at the same time and knit them in the same row automatically. The punchcard determined which colour was knitted on which needle. Machines were commonly used in the homes of machine knitters in the Shetland Islands to increase the speed of production for time-consuming garments. A system developed of out-workers machine knitting bodies and sleeves that were then passed to hand knitters to complete with hand-knitted patterned yokes. In fact, it is still common today that knitters in the islands will design and knit their samples on a machine before translating the pattern to hand knit so that it is accessible to a wider audience.

Marie Bruhat designs and knits traditional Fair Isle garments from her studio on Fair Isle.

Political sweaters from Lisa Anne Auerbach.

Sophie Ochera uses a standard gauge knitting machine to produce the main body of all her knitwear.

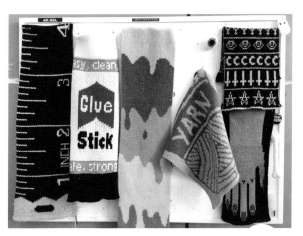

Playful designs from Kandy Diamond at Knit and Destroy.

But where hand knitting has gone before, machine knitting is following and there is a new and revived interest in being able to speed up the knitting process by using machines to help with the laborious parts. As well as this, there are a growing band of hand knitters who want to add to their repertoire and learn to machine knit too so they can knit both more productively but also techniques or types of yarn and fabric that simply aren't possible to work easily by hand. More and more knitters are coming round to the benefits of being able to do both, even combining hand and machine knitting in the same garment.

And not just in traditional ways: even though there is a happy growth of machine knitters designing and selling traditional Fair Isle designs, there is also a growing trend for designers to use their machines and their creativity to design new, exciting and challenging designs. The immediacy of machine knitting gives them a greater opportunity to try out ideas and get them in front of people, keeping pace with fashion trends and political movements.

THIS BOOK

Knitting machines are very robust and long-lasting pieces of equipment and many machine knitters today are happily knitting away with machines that are up to fifty years old. In today's world of built-in obsolescence these machines are even more relevant as they can still produce just as amazing knitwear as the newest domestic machines. This book is aimed at those using punchcard machines, which will cover the majority of these older models, as well as brand-new punchcard machines that can still be bought today. Technology has advanced some makes and models and there are now many machines that have an electronic patterning component that offers more freedom with pattern designing. Knitters using any of the electronic machines (both vintage and brand new) can still get full benefit from this book in conjunction with the manual for your individual software. It is simply unfeasible for one book to cover all the permutations and advancements in software technology (and it would date very quickly) but all the techniques and patterns that I cover here will work perfectly on an electronic machine as well.

It is also applicable to all makes of Japanese domestic flat-bed machines with a punchcard facility. On the whole, I will talk about Silver Reed and Brother machines and explain any key differences between the two. There are several other smaller brands that are still in common use but generally they will operate in the same way as one of these two. This covers the majority of machines used by machine knitters today. The main thing to start with is the instruction manual that came with your machine.

Silver Reed is the only make of knitting machine that is still widely available to buy as new today. This is the latest brand name for the company which in the past has produced, amongst others, Knitmaster, Empisal, Singer, and Studio. In this book when I refer to Silver Reed machines I am referring to any of the brand names that fall under this banner.

The book is aimed primarily at newer machine knitters who want to learn how to use punchcards to knit Fair Isle for the first time, but it is also appropriate for machine knitters who have mastered the basics but are looking for the knowledge and confidence to develop their machine knitting skills further.

If this has left you feeling fired up to get to grips with Fair Isle knitting on your own punchcard machine, then this is just the book for you.

For the purposes of this book, if you have a Knitmaster machine like this one you should follow instructions for Silver Reed machines.

I use Knitmaster and Silver Reed machines but where relevant the book will show separate instructions for Brother machines like this one.

CHAPTER 1

TWO-COLOUR FAIR ISLE: THE BASICS

When you acquire your very first knitting machine there is a lot to learn. Even though the machine can help with speed, efficiency and productivity, it still needs to be operated by somebody who knows what they are doing, and it can be a steep learning curve to get to that stage. Much time will be spent, with an instruction manual, initially learning how to cast on and off and achieve perfect stitches and tension. Once this is mastered, the next thing that most new machine knitters will want to get to grips with is the punchcard facility, which will help them to create automated patterns far more easily than by hand knitting.

HOW DOES A KNITTING MACHINE WORK?

Before you can understand how the punchcard works in operating the machine, it is important to understand how the needles and needle positions on your machine work in general.

How a latch needle works

The simple but clever latch needle is the foundation for all knitting machines and the stitches and fabric that they produce. Even though different brands and types of knitting machine will have different sizes and types of needle they will all still work on the same principle to construct stitches every time the carriage moves over them.

When a needle is selected to be in work and has been cast-on it will hold one stitch in the hook of the needle and the latch will close over the top of it to hold it in place. Every time the carriage moves over the needle it will move forward, opening the latch and pushing the original stitch back behind it.

The latch tool is simply a latch needle with a handle.

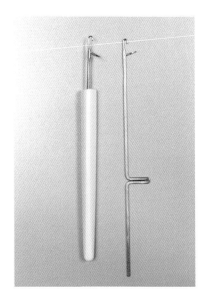

At the same time, the carriage will thread the main yarn into the now empty hook, closing the latch and then it will push the needle back, pulling the new yarn through the original stitch leaving a newly created stitch back in the hook. This process repeats for every single pass of the carriage.

Whenever I am teaching new machine knitters, I start by explaining and demonstrating this process because once you understand it, it will help you to comprehend and rectify one of the most common early mistakes: dropped stitches. But it will also help you to understand exactly what is happening when you start to use your punchcard facility too.

STEP-BY-STEP: HOW A STITCH IS FORMED

1. Original stitch held in hook of the needle.

2. Carriage moves over the needle.

3. Needle moves forward and stitch falls behind the latch.

4. Carriage feeds the yarn into the empty hook.

5. Needle moves back into position, pulling the yarn through the original stitch.

6. A new stitch is formed.

Understanding needle positions

The second thing that every machine knitter needs to understand, particularly to use punchcards successfully, is the different options available for needle positions and what impact they have.

At the end of your needle bed, there will be a set of letters in different positions. The letters will be different depending on the make of your machine but generally Silver Reed will be A–D and Brother machines will have letters A, B, D & E.

Brother needle positions are A, B, D or E.

Needle positions on Silver Reed machines are A, B, C or D.

THE FOUR BASIC NEEDLE POSITIONS

A = non-working position

This is a resting position for your needles and if they stay here they will never move when the carriage runs over them. We refer to these needles as being 'out of work'. It is good practice to always move your needles back to this position when you have completed a piece of knitting.

B = working position

This is the most commonly used position for your knitting. When you are starting a new piece of knitting by casting on you will select the needles you want to use by pushing them to B position. You can move them either manually with your finger or using the needle pusher supplied with your machine. Any needle that is in B position will create a new stitch every time the carriage passes over it, as long as there is also yarn in the feeder.

C or D = upper working position

This is a much less-frequently used position and is a way of moving needles back into work after they have been in holding position. If a needle is pushed back into this position it will knit back to B the next time the carriage passes over it with yarn in the feeder. Be careful not to push it too far back though: if it goes all the way back to B the last stitch will drop off the needle.

D or E = holding position

Holding position is a really useful function for a variety of techniques including shaping in garments as well as short-row shaping. When your needles are in D or E position and you have your Hold levers on your carriage set to Hold then they will remain in that position every time the carriage moves across even if it has yarn in the feeder. Your instruction manual will have full details of how this works. We will cover how you can use this position in relation to Fair Isle knitting in Chapter 6.

HOW DOES A PUNCHCARD MACHINE WORK?

All of the previous information on needles and needle positions should help you to understand how knitting is formed on a knitting machine and will allow you to create plain stocking stitch fabric. But the real excitement comes from using a punchcard to manipulate needles and their positions automatically to create fancy patterned stitches, such as tuck and slip or, as is the focus for this book, two-colour patterned Fair Isle knitting.

All punchcard knitting machines are originally sold with a set of pre-punched punchcards that can be used for a variety of patterned stitches. If you have acquired your machine second hand and

the punchcards have been lost, they are widely and cheaply available online. In Chapter 5, we will explore how you can design and produce your own punchcards.

A punchcard is a plastic card with a series of holes and blanks that programme each of the needles on a machine to either 'knit' or 'not knit'. For Fair Isle knitting, the programme will tell all the needles to knit, but either 'knit colour A' or 'knit colour B'. For standard-gauge knitting machines the card patterning will be 24 stitches wide. On the majority of chunky machines it is 12 stitches and usually for fine gauge machines it is 36 stitches but it will vary between make and model, so check your manual. For example, Brother chunky machines also use the 24-stitch repeat.

When a punchcard is in position and your carriage is set for Fair Isle, every time the carriage passes the punchcard reader it will pick up the 'needle programme' ready to knit the relevant pattern on the next row.

Unless you set the machine for motif knitting, the machine will repeat the Fair Isle patterning over all the needles in work and over every row, until you cancel the programming. In this chapter we will explore creating an all-over Fair Isle pattern. We will cover motif knitting and how to knit Fair Isle just in certain areas of your knitting in Chapter 4.

UNDERSTANDING AND READING YOUR PUNCHCARD

One of the things new knitters struggle with when using punchcards for the first time is understanding exactly what a punchcard will do, and when and how to start it. It can also sometimes be difficult to look at a punchcard pattern and visualize exactly how it will look in a patterned stitch. This is especially true with tuck or slip stitch. It is easier with Fair Isle as most people can look at the pattern and imagine it

A standard punchcard for a Silver Reed machine.

in two colours, but it is still hard to visualize it in four, five or six different colours. However, there can still be a lot to understand or read from the card and it's always worth taking a few minutes to look at it before setting off knitting for the first time.

Your card will be made up of a series of holes and blanks. The carriage will move needles into different needle positions accordingly. The blanks will correspond with needles that will knit the main colour (the yarn in yarn feeder 1) and the holes correspond with needles that will knit the contrast colour (the yarn in feeder 2).

On each side of the card there will be two guide holes. These are for your card clips so that you can join the ends of your card and turn it into a continuous loop.

At the top and bottom of each card there will be two rows of continuous holes. These are not part of the pattern; they simply allow the pattern to repeat continuously once it has been joined in a loop.

The most important thing to understand is the numbering up the side of the card. It should read from number 1 through to XX (depending on the length of your card). But you will notice that it doesn't start with 1 at the bottom. On Brother cards the 1 will be seven positions higher and on Silver Reed it will be five positions higher. When you want

to start a new punchcard you will feed it into your card reader and position it so that row 1 is showing as the next row. But the pattern the machine is actually programming will be 5 or 7 rows below inside the card reader. The first row of holes and blanks that are visible to you will actually be knitted in five or seven rows' time (see photos below).

You will also notice the letters A to D in the bottom corner front and back on the card. This refers to the direction of the card. A punchcard can be fed into the reader in four different directions. If the pattern on the card is symmetrical it will make no difference which way round you feed it. But if you have a pattern that has an important direction (such as letters) then you need to make sure you are inserting the card in the right direction.

Once you understand all of this, there should be no surprises with the swatch you are knitting from your chosen card.

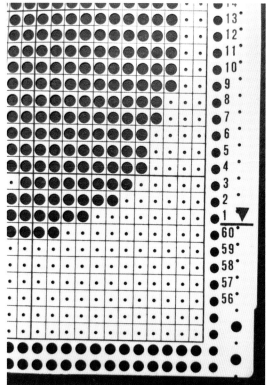

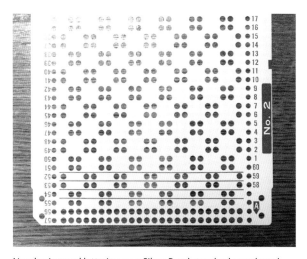

Numbering and lettering on a Silver Reed standard punchcard.

Numbering and lettering on a Brother standard punchcard.

THE PUNCHCARD READER OR PATTERN PANEL

This is the 'computer' on your machine that will be programming all the needles to knit the colours you want it to. The reader will take the holes on your card and transfer these to the carriage which will then select the appropriate needles for each colour.

The pattern reader or panel itself though is surprisingly basic. You will have a dial for feeding your punchcard into the machine along with a selector for locking and unlocking the card and choosing between short/standard and long stitch. We will look at the variations between standard and long stitch in Chapter 2. For this chapter we will only be looking at standard stitch.

SETTING UP YOUR CARRIAGE FOR FAIR ISLE KNITTING

Whenever you are setting up your machine for specific techniques, I would recommend that you have your instruction manual to hand. There are so many varieties of make and model that it is impossible to cover all the nuances in a book and it is always good practice to refer to your instruction manual in the first instance. If you no longer have the manual for your machine, they can be downloaded for free from the Internet. But the principles outlined below will explain what functions on your carriage you need to focus on for Fair Isle knitting.

Silver Reed machines

See the diagram of the carriage with all the relevant functions labelled. These functions work in the following way.

Silver Reed card reader.

Brother card reader.

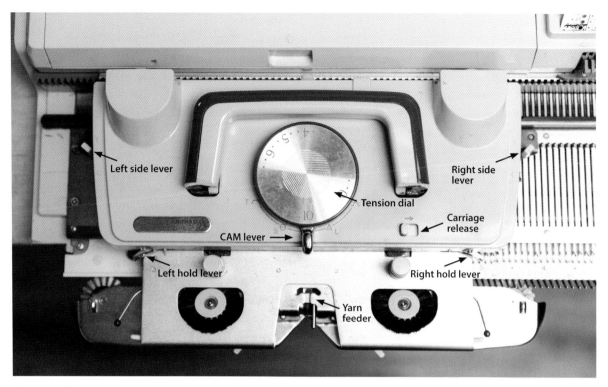

The carriage from a Silver Reed machine.

Tension dial

Officially this dial is your 'stitch size' dial but it is more commonly referred to as your tension dial. If a pattern calls for you to knit in a certain tension, then this is the dial it is referring to. It will be numbered from 0 through to 10 with 0 being the tightest or smallest stitch and 10 being the loosest or largest. You change this dial depending on the type of yarn you are using and the type of stitch you want to create.

Setting the cam lever

This lever at the bottom of your tension dial selects the type of knitting you want to use. For regular stocking stitch the lever is in the middle on ^. Depending on the age of your machine there will be more or fewer options for alternative cam settings, but for Fair Isle you always need to use setting F. When you have finished Fair Isle knitting it's really

important that you remember to change your cam back to plain knitting otherwise you will have problems with dropped stitches and ladders. In the worst cases, your entire knitting will fall to the floor!

Side levers

These levers on your machine are commonly overlooked or misunderstood and are rarely explained properly in your instruction manual. I like to think of them as an on/off lever as they are telling the carriage to either perform the technique you have asked (on) or not (off). The one on the left-hand side controls the function when the carriage is moving from right to left; the right-hand switch controls the carriage moving from left to right. For any punchcard knitting you need to make sure both of these levers are set to 'On' – which is towards the back – otherwise they will ignore the punchcard and carry on plain knitting.

Holding levers

As mentioned when we covered needle positions, these levers control what happens to any needles that are in D position. For Fair Isle knitting generally you need to make sure both of these are set to || or 'not hold'. The exception to this is when you want to knit Fair Isle just in certain portions of your knitting and we will cover this in more detail in Chapters 4 and 6.

Carriage release

This is your get-out-of-jail switch! If your carriage gets jammed or you run into problems in the middle of a row this switch will allow you to flip the carriage open and run it along the remainder of the row without knitting (or dropping) any stitches. You can then rectify any problems before clicking your carriage back down into position and beginning again. On some older machines your carriage release will be less obvious or work slightly differently so it is always worth checking this in your instruction manual.

Yarn feeder

Your yarn feeder will have two numbers marked on the carriage arm: 1 and 2 with a gate in between. If you have never knitted Fair Isle before, you will only ever have used feeder 1 which is for the main colour. When knitting Fair Isle you feed your main colour into this feeder, close the gate and add the contrast colour in front of the gate in feeder 2. It is important to make sure that both colours are fed in cleanly and into the correct holes. Once these are both secured and your carriage is set to Fair Isle, it will select the appropriate colour for each needle automatically.

Brother machines

See the diagram of the carriage with all the relevant functions labelled. Many of the functions work in exactly the same way as for Silver Reed machines but they will be in different places or be called different things. Below are the functions that you need to understand on your carriage.

Tension dial

This dial changes your stitch size. It will be numbered from 0 through to 10 with 0 being the tightest or smallest stitch and 10 being the loosest or largest. You change this dial depending on the type of yarn you are using and the type of stitch you want to create.

Cam buttons

These buttons are in the centre of your carriage beneath the tension dial and they select the type of knitting you want to use. There are two on the left for Tuck, two on the right for Slip (Part) and the centre button, MC, is the one you need for Fair Isle. To knit Fair Isle you push the MC button in. For regular stocking stitch you need to cancel any of these buttons by pushing the cam button release lever which will be labelled 'Plain'. When you have finished Fair Isle knitting it's really important that you remember to cancel the MC button otherwise you will have problems with dropped stitches and ladders. In the worst cases, your entire knitting will fall to the floor!

Change knob

This dial will normally be set to N-L for plain knitting. When you are knitting Fair Isle you need to make sure this is turned to KC to switch Fair Isle patterning on. When you go back to plain knitting you need to make sure that this dial is turned back to N-L. Also on the dial are SM (single motif) and CR (carriage release). We're not covering single motif knitting in this chapter but your CR function can be very helpful for getting you out of trouble! If your carriage gets jammed or you run into problems in the middle of a row this dial will allow you to lift the carriage off the machine. You can then rectify any problems before clicking your carriage back down onto the end of the bed and switching back to N-L and beginning again.

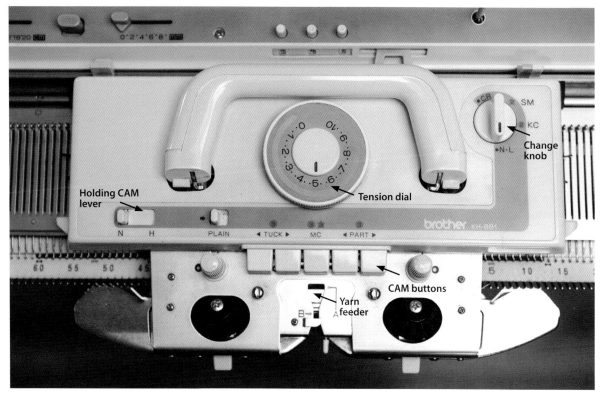

The carriage from a Brother machine.

Holding cam lever

For Fair Isle knitting generally you need to make sure this is on N for 'not hold'. The exception to this is when you want to knit Fair Isle just in certain portions of your knitting. We will cover this in Chapters 4 and 6.

Yarn feeder

Your yarn feeder will have two letters marked on the carriage arm: A and B with a gate in between. If you have never knitted Fair Isle before you will only ever have used feeder A which is for the main colour. When knitting Fair Isle you feed your main colour into this feeder, close the gate and add the contrast colour in front of the gate in feeder B. It is important to make sure that both colours are fed in cleanly and into the correct holes. Once these

are both secured and your carriage MC cam button is selected, it will choose the appropriate colour for each needle automatically.

End needle selection

This setting is unique to later versions of Brother machines (and is also an option for any machines using DesignaKnit software). It is designed to create a more secure edge stitch and eradicate gaps between colour changes in your pattern. It will mean that the first stitch on every row will always be the contrast colour stitch. You need it switched on for Fair Isle and this is done by moving two cams on the underneath of the carriage. Check your instruction manual to see if this is a feature of your machine and how to turn it on. We will cover end needle selection in more detail in Chapter 4.

It's useful to have all the following tools to hand for Fair Isle knitting:

Pre-punched punchcards
For your first Fair Isle practice swatches you will need the punchcards that came with your machine. If you don't have any, you can order more via the Internet.

Card clips
For securing your cards into a continuous piece that can keep rotating through the punchcard feeder.

Transfer tools and latch tool
I always have these in a pot whenever I am working at my machine. Even if you are not using them for shaping or moving stitches around, they are useful for catching and picking up dropped stitches and putting them back on the needles.

Scissors
Some newer machines have a yarn cutter on the carriage arm. Otherwise you will need scissors for cutting yarns as you change colours.

The basic tools for Fair Isle knitting.

Notebook and pen
I would highly recommend having these to hand for noting all the details about anything you are knitting. They are particularly helpful when you are working on swatches or trial pieces so you can make write down all the details such as number of needles, rows, stitch size, yarn and tension. There is nothing more annoying than creating a beautiful swatch and not having a note of how you made it.

YARNS FOR FAIR ISLE KNITTING

Choosing your yarns and colours
Half the fun of coloured patterned knitting is choosing yarns and colours to knit together and everybody will have their own personal preferences. In theory, your choices are unlimited but for Fair Isle there are certain types of yarn and colour combinations that will work better than others.

In traditional Fair Isle you would always use the same make of yarn for both the main and contrast colour. Shetland yarn is the standard choice for this type of knitting as it has a fluffy, woolly texture that helps the stitches bed together and creates a nice stable pattern and texture. But really interesting effects can be achieved by combining yarns of different structures and thicknesses.

Equally, your choice of colour can have a surprising impact on the finished look. Ideally you are looking for two colours that contrast well against each other but you can choose very bright colours or more muted, tonal shades and the same pattern will look very different. In traditional Fair Isle knitting it is the colour combinations and number of changes and variations that give it such a distinct and striking look.

We will investigate how you can design and practise different colourways in Chapter 5 but for the practice pieces at the end of this chapter, you can have fun practising with spare yarns that you have available and seeing what effect that has. If you are new to machine knitting or Fair Isle knitting I would suggest starting with more standard yarns, that knit easily in your machine; also, try and choose two yarns that are the same or very similar. Then as

Fair Isle swatches in alternative yarns.

The same Fair Isle pattern can look quite different just by alternating colours.

you become more experienced start to play around and see what a difference it makes.

Threading yarns into your machine

Your instruction manual will give you details of how to thread your yarn through your yarn mast and down into the yarn feeder. Make sure you follow these instructions carefully and have your machine set up with the first two colours you want to use for your Fair Isle pattern. We have talked already about the stitch size/tension dial on the carriage of your machine and this is an important factor but you will also see that you have tension discs at the top of your yarn mast, which also control the tension of your knitting. Refer to your instruction manual to make sure you understand how these will impact your knitting as well.

Selecting the correct tension

When you are knitting Fair Isle for the first time, it will be difficult to judge exactly what tension to use for your knitting and there will be an element of trial and error. There are a few things to consider.

In any Fair Isle knitting you will be using double the thickness of yarn across the bed of your machine so it is often recommended to make your stitch size one whole number higher than you would do for standard stocking stitch in a single yarn. But your choice of yarn will also be an important factor. Some will knit Fair Isle more easily than others and some will be more temperamental. Again, a lot of this understanding will come with experience and the best way to learn about this is to keep practising with different swatches in different yarn types.

Finally, if you are knitting with coned yarns that are specifically sold as machine knitting yarns they will more than likely be oiled, to run through the machines more easily. This is great for improving the ease of knitting. But you need to remember that when you wash them for the first time, the oil will be removed and the nature of your stitches will alter. On the whole the yarns will 'fluff up' after washing and many knitters refer to this as 'blooming'. They also develop a much softer, nicer hand feel at this stage. You need to remember this when selecting your ideal tension as you want to allow room between the stitches for this blooming. So you will often aim for a tension that looks a little bit airy so that when the knitting is washed, all the stitches will bloom and fill the gaps beautifully without feeling too stiff.

There is a lot to take in when you are practising Fair Isle for the first time but the very best way to get to grips with it is by practising swatches until you increase your confidence and experience.

The swatches below have been taken from the Silver Reed standard gauge set so you should have something similar available to you. If you don't have the exact one that I have chosen, don't worry. Almost all of the pre-punched cards that you have can be used. In your instruction manual there will be a table that tells you if a card is suitable for Fair Isle, as there will be a few that aren't.

A selection of two-colour swatches using a standard Silver Reed punchcard.

Switching Fair Isle on and off

The key thing to understand is *when* to switch settings on and off. This comes back to the point I made earlier about the machine picking up or reading the pattern the row prior to actually knitting it. So you have to think about setting up your machine at least one row prior as well. It works slightly differently for different makes of machine but the basic principles to remember are described below.

Silver Reed

Your carriage needs to have moved past the card reader at least once, when the card is in there and locked in the start position, for the pattern to be picked up and transferred to the carriage. When you lock your card in position the teeth underneath will move to show you the pattern it has picked up. This is what will be transferred to the carriage and knitted as soon as you select Fair Isle. As good practice I always try and put my card into the reader and lock it ready in position before I even cast on; then I know for sure that the carriage will have gone past at least once. If you forget, it doesn't matter. You can still feed your card in and lock it in position. If you want patterning to start on the very next row you will need to move your carriage across without any yarn in it, using Carriage Release so that the stitches don't drop off. Or you can add yarn and knit at least one more row of plain knitting before you start.

Once you have picked up the pattern on the carriage you can set your carriage to knit Fair Isle by selecting 'F' on your cam lever, adding both yarns

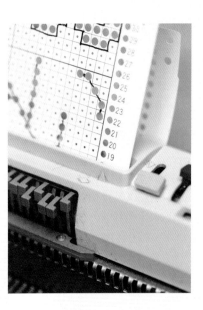

On a Silver Reed machine, teeth on the feeder show the patterning when it is locked in position.

into Feeder 1 and 2 and unlocking the card. Now every row you knit will knit Fair Isle and the card will rotate by one position until you cancel Fair Isle knitting.

To cancel you simply lock your card, change your cam lever back to stocking stitch and remove your second colour. You can now continue with plain knitting.

See the step-by-step instructions below for the full run-through.

STEP-BY-STEP: SWITCHING FAIR ISLE ON AND OFF (SILVER REED)

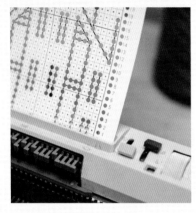

1. Insert punchcard, rotate to start point and lock in position.

2. Knit at least one row with yarn or a free pass with no yarn.

3. Change cam lever to F.

4. Add second colour to Feeder 2.

5. Release punchcard.

6. Push first needle out to D position.

...continued on next page

…continued from previous page

7. Start knitting rows in Fair Isle and continue until you have completed your Fair Isle pattern. NOTE: Make sure the carriage moves at least 5cm past the Pattern Panel and at least 2cm past each end of the knitting.

8. Lock card in position.

9. Change cam lever back to plain knitting ^.

10. Remove second colour from Feeder 2.

11. Continue with plain knitting.

Brother

Brother punchcards work in a different way to pick up the patterning but they still need to be 'set up' the row before you want to start patterning. Again, you need to make sure your card is in the reader and locked in position. On the row before you want to start Fair Isle you need to change your Change Knob to K-C and knit one plain row. This will pick up the pattern and move the relevant needles into position ready for Fair Isle knitting on the next row. At this stage you then select your 'MC' cam button, release your card and add both yarns into the feeder and you can start Fair Isle knitting.

To cancel, lock your card, remove the second colour, cancel your MC button and turn your Change Knob to N-L. You can now continue with plain knitting.

See the step-by-step instructions below for the full run-through.

STEP-BY-STEP: SWITCHING FAIR ISLE ON AND OFF (BROTHER)

1. Insert punchcard and rotate to start point and lock in position.

2. Switch Change Knob to 'KC' one row before you want to start Fair Isle and knit one row plain knit. The selected needles will move out to D position.

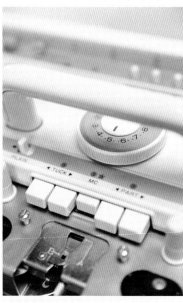

3. Change cam button to MC and add second colour to Feeder B.

…continued on next page

...continued from previous page

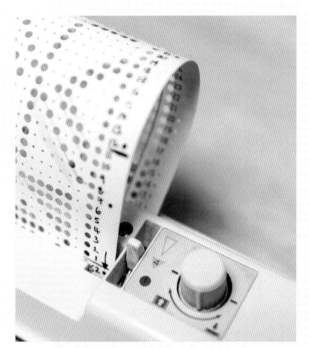

4. Release punchcard and start knitting rows in Fair Isle and continue until you have completed your Fair Isle pattern. NOTE: Make sure the carriage moves at least 2cm past each end of the knitting.

5. Lock card in position.

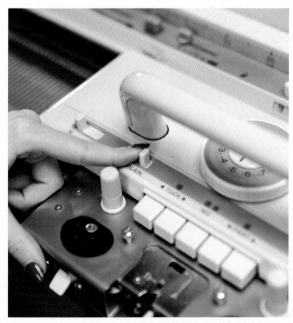

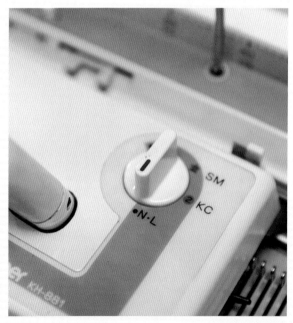

6. Cancel MC cam button.

7. Turn Change Knob to N-L. Remove second colour from Feeder 2 and continue with plain knitting.

Practising and evaluating your swatches

One of the things that separates experienced machine knitters from novices is the intuitive understanding of what a difference changing yarns, colours and tensions in a piece of knitting can make. This can be one of the most frustrating things when you are new to machine knitting as you simply don't know which yarns will be better for certain types of knitting and you can end up spending a lot of wasted time struggling with yarns or techniques that somebody more advanced would have discounted immediately. Equally, newer knitters sometimes lack the confidence to try anything more than the exact instructions they are given because they are worried about doing the wrong thing or breaking the machine (which is very unlikely to happen). Unfortunately, the only way inexperienced knitters can get past this stage is to start practising and building up experience and knowledge; the best way you can speed up this process is by assessing each of your swatches as you go along. This is why evaluation is such an important part of the learning process.

Once you have knitted your first swatch, start to play around with all of the important variables such as yarn type, colours, and stitch size with more swatches. This will also help you to familiarize yourself with all the controls and practise the techniques at the same time.

Changing tension

This is the quickest and easiest change to try. You can keep exactly the same colours threaded up and try making the stitch size smaller or larger. Think about how this feels when you move the carriage across. If it starts to feel stiff and hard to move then your stitch size is becoming too small. If the knitting becomes really loose and lacey then it is probably too large but consider the comments below about blocking and measuring as well.

Changing colours

The other simple change to make is to switch colour combinations. In one swatch you might try really contrasting colours whereas in another you might choose colours that are closer and just differ tonally. You might even be surprised what a difference you will see by using the same two colours and switching them between main colour and contrast colour. When I am working on a new design or pattern I quite often knit a really long panel of swatches with the same pattern and yarn but switching between a number of colour combinations to see which works best. Sometimes a combination you are convinced will work really well when you see the cones next to each other, doesn't have quite the right mix when it is knitted in the pattern. And a lot of this will also come down to personal preference and favourite colours too.

A swatch of my 'Hebden Houses' pattern in different colour options.

Using different types of yarn

In this case, more than the previous two, be prepared for some unsuccessful swatches. Start trying to mix yarns that are very different in structure: perhaps a very fluffy yarn with a very crisp one; or thick with thin. Some of these will work better than others, both aesthetically and technically. But you will begin to see what a difference it can make. And be prepared to accept that sometimes your machine (or you!) simply won't like some of the combinations.

Washing and blocking

Whole books have been written on this subject and so I'm not going to go into full detail here. But when evaluating any of your machine knitting (swatches or full garments) it is always important to wash and block them to create a professional finish. You might think this unnecessary for a pile of swatches but you won't be able to evaluate them properly and use them successfully unless you know what they will look like once they are finished. And it can make quite a difference to the appearance and the hand feel. As explained earlier, yarns that have been oiled specifically for machine knitting can alter dramatically as the oil is removed and the fibre blooms. You might even find that the colours change as well.

You will also need to go through this process if you are developing your swatches further to use them in full garments when you will need tension squares. So it is definitely a good habit to develop. If you are unsure how to go about this, there are plenty of free tutorials available online explaining the details. I have included details in the Further Resources section at the end of this book. We will also cover this in more detail in Chapter 3.

Recording information and storing your swatches

The most important thing to remember when you are having fun knitting lots of swatches is to record the details so you can repeat it again if you want to. As I mentioned previously, it can be very annoying

It's always a good idea to label your swatches with as many details as possible.

to find a swatch you knitted a while ago and would love to use for a new garment only to realize that you don't have any details about how you created it in the first place. It doesn't have to be anything complicated at this stage but here are a few of the things that I always try to record:

- Yarn supplier and name
- Yarn weight and colours
- Machine used
- Number of stitches and rows in the swatch
- Tension/stitch size
- Reference to the punchcard used

People have different methods for recording and storing the information but I find the quickest and easiest way is to use small tags that can be attached to the swatch. You can have a dedicated notebook or spreadsheet for logging them or use labels that are stuck or pinned to the swatch. Some people even use systems to knit a code into each swatch. The main thing is to come up with something that works for you and that you can always find whenever you need to know how you knitted that beautiful swatch you are now ready to use.

A pile of beautiful swatches for future inspiration and projects.

Evaluation

Once you have been through this process you can decide which swatches you want to keep and which are unsuccessful. If you want to fast track your understanding, try to dig deep, and decide what it is you like about some swatches and dislike about others. If there are swatches that aren't any good, what is it that makes them unappealing? The more questions and answers you come up with, the more you will begin to build up knowledge, experience and confidence. Any unsuccessful swatches can be pulled back and the yarn re-used for swatching another time. Your aim is to start building up a library of gorgeous swatches that you can come back to for future inspiration and projects.

CHAPTER 2

VARIATIONS ON THE SAME PUNCHCARD

S ome of the punchcards you receive with your machine might look quite simple and it's easy to think that you can only really produce one design from each card. But this couldn't be further from the truth. In fact, each card offers almost limitless permutations for the end result. We will cover how you can really push Fair Isle designs to the limit in Chapter 6, but in this chapter we will cover some of the standard options you can vary to create different effects. If you like, you can go back to using your punchcard from Chapter 1 and practise more swatches using the following adaptations or choose a different one and see which you prefer.

looks the same both upside down or flipped sideways. But if you imagine the punchcard contained some lettering or a non-symmetrical pattern then it will look different depending on which version of the card that you use.

The majority of the standard cards are designed symmetrically but if you can find one that isn't, then experiment with changing the direction and see what happens. This is a more important consideration once you move onto designing your own Fair Isle patterns, which we will cover in more detail in Chapter 5.

VARIATION 1: CARD PLACEMENT AND DIRECTION

If you look at any of your pre-punched cards, you will notice there are two letters in the corner on each side of the card: A and C on one side and B and D on the reverse. Each of the letters appear in a small box arrow indicating the direction for the card. If you place the card into the pattern reader with A at the bottom right, then you will be knitting Version A of the card. If you turn it over and feed it in with D at the bottom right, then you are knitting pattern version D. For a pattern that is symmetrical in both directions (horizontal and vertical) this will have no impact on the knitted piece as the pattern

This punchcard pattern is asymmetrical and so looks different depending which way you use it.

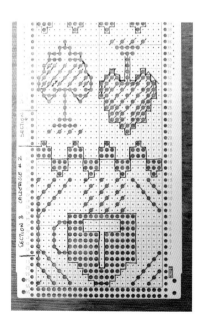

VARIATION 2: INTRODUCING MULTIPLE COLOURS

In Chapter 1 we looked at using just two colours (a main colour and a contrast colour) for the full pattern. But there is no reason why you can't switch these around or even introduce new colours as you knit more rows. Indeed, this is often preferred in order to make the design more pleasing. Think about traditional Fair Isle patterns where the colours change continually, sometimes every three to five rows. Switching between background and foreground colour in a Fair Isle pattern can also be an interesting technique to break up what might otherwise be a monotonous design.

If you have ever knitted stripes in plain knitting then you will be familiar with the technique of changing colours in Feeder 1. It becomes a little fiddlier and needs a little bit more attention when you are alternating or changing between more than two colours in both feeders, often at the same time. Practice will definitely help, but the following tips should also be considered.

Alternating Colour A and Colour B

If you want to continue with the same two colours, but alternate which is the main and contrast colour, it is quite easy to switch these over but you need to be careful not to twist your yarns or get them tangled in the underneath of your carriage as you do it. I find that the safest way to do this is to remove both yarns from the feeder entirely and let the tension mast pull them straight back up to the yarn mast; then take your new main colour and place that in the feeder, close the gate, and now add the new contrast colour. Double-check both yarns are in the correct parts of the feeder cleanly and that any gates are closed before re-starting. It is quite easy to do this switch quickly, or without concentrating fully, and miss one of the feeders and you end up with dropped stitches or the entire piece of knitting on the floor.

Introducing new colour(s)

When you want to introduce multiple colours into your patterning, you will need to remove one or both of your original colours entirely. If you are changing only one of the colours you would do this in exactly the same way as when you are changing colours for stripes. But all the same words of caution remain from above: make sure that yarns aren't twisted and that they are fed cleanly into the feeders.

Cutting vs. carrying colour up the side

Quite often you might end up removing and reintroducing several colours, multiple times. Depending on whether the colour you are removing will be used again further up the pattern you can either cut the yarn at this stage, leaving an end long enough to be woven in, or you can choose to rest it at the side of

Notice how the colour changes in the background of this Fair Isle pattern.

The side clip on this Silver Reed machine is designed to hold yarn out of the way.

Carry the yarn up the side of the knitting by hooking it in the hook of the needle before knitting the next row.

your machine. Many machines have side clips at each end of the bed for exactly this purpose.

If you decide to place the yarn at the side whilst you continue knitting, then you will want to 'carry' this yarn up the side of the knitting as you knit. All this means is that you hook the yarn into the hook of the needle every alternate row and it will be knitted in to the end stitch leaving you a nice, neat selvedge on your knitting.

The decision will usually depend on how many rows there are before you will be re-introducing the colour. If it is less than six rows, then I would carry the yarn up rather than cutting it and giving yourself more ends to deal with.

Optional use of a colour changer and/or multiple yarn masts

For very complicated Fair Isle patterns with multiple colours it can be quite cumbersome to have to keep removing and adding yarns into your yarn masts every time that they change. In these cases, it is preferable to have more yarn masts so that you can have several yarns permanently set up at the same time. Second-hand yarn masts are quite easy to source, and many machines have the ability to hold a second yarn mast. This gives you the option of having four colours set up at any one time. Some people who knit with a lot of colours on a regular basis choose to adapt their machine knitting tables

Traditional Fair Isle patterns often use several different colours that change every few rows.

so that they can hold even more masts. Or you have the option of purchasing a colour changer as an accessory for your machine. You will need to investigate the exact model that works with your particular machine, but these are a useful option when working with up to four colours at any one time and they give you the ability to switch between the colours in Feeder 2 at the tap of a button. Remember, though, that colour changers rely on you changing colour on the same side of the bed each time and this is often not the case for traditional Fair Isle patterns. At the end of the day your choices will come down to personal use and how often you think you will be using more than two colours on a regular basis.

VARIATION 3: LOCKING YOUR CARD IN POSITION

When you followed the instructions in Chapter 1 for knitting your first swatch, one of the steps was to 'unlock' your card before you started knitting. This meant that the card would rotate one position every time your carriage moved across the bed. But you can still knit Fair Isle with the card locked and it will simply repeat the same patterning row every time until you unlock it again. In fact, this can quite often happen unintentionally when you forget to unlock your card, and can lead to some interesting variations to a pattern. For example, it is a useful way of creating vertical stripes in machine knitting. You can also play around with locking and unlocking your card at various stages in the patterning to create more variety to the original design.

VARIATION 4: VARYING THE LENGTH OF YOUR PATTERN

Punchcard machines all have a facility to double the length of your pattern. Instead of advancing the card by one position every time the carriage moves across the bed, it will only advance every alternate row, thus doubling the length of the pattern. As with the previous variation, you can experiment by lengthening your pattern in certain places and not in others to create more variety to the design. On Silver Reed machines this is operated by your S/L lever (S = short and L = long) and on Brother machines you have a triangle that indicates Intermittent Card Feeding on your Card Lock Lever. Consult your machine's manual for specific instructions.

A Knitmaster machine setup with two yarn masts gives it the ability to have four different colours threaded up at the same time.

Here the pattern has been switched between every row and alternate rows for the card rotation.

Can you spot the sections in this pattern where the punchcard was locked on one row?

Cowl and wrist warmer knitted with a combination of four different colours and alternating short and long patterning.

Wrist warmers are designed to keep your hands warm whilst you can still use your fingers.

Now that you have fully tested a punchcard and experimented with the most common variations on the same card you are probably eager to progress from swatches to completing your first fully finished piece of Fair Isle knitting. The following pattern is for a matching set of wrist warmers and a cowl. This is a quick and easy introduction into using punchcards as there is no shaping to worry about at this stage; we are simply knitting rectangles and joining them together. If you like, think of it as larger swatches.

This pattern will test everything you have learnt so far and if you feel confident enough you can personalize it further by incorporating some of the adaptations discussed earlier in this chapter.

Yarn
⬥ J.C. Rennie 2/11.3Nm Supersoft 100% lambswool (equivalent to 4 ply hand knitting weight)

⬥ 250g total across four colours (this allows adequate for practice swatches and tension squares)
  ⬥ Col A = 379 Mole
  ⬥ Col B = 199 Nutmeg
  ⬥ Col C = 37 Calypso
  ⬥ Col D = 340 Rosebud

Knitting machine
Knitted on a standard gauge Knitmaster 360.

Punchcard pattern chart
The pattern is worked using Silver Reed Card No. 3 and uses four colours for the patterning. But feel free to replace this with the punchcard of your choice and mix the colours up if you like. Sometimes it's fun to alternate the colours across the garments as in my example here. (See the Appendix at the back of the book for copies of all the punchcards used.)

Tension

◇ 34 sts and 38 rows to 10cm (4in) in Fair Isle pattern. Tension dial at T6.

Size and finished measurements

◇ One size
◇ Wrist warmers: 9.5cm wide x 18.5cm long
◇ Cowl: 28cm wide x 112cm long

Colour charts

See the Appendix at the back of the book for colour charts.

Pattern instructions

Wrist warmers (make two)

The pattern below is written to include a rib cuff at the bottom. If you do not have a ribber, or are unconfident knitting rib, then you can simply start with an e-wrap cast on using your main bed only and knit 10 rows of stocking stitch in MC A before continuing the pattern. This will give you a nice rolled edge instead.

Instruction	Tension	Needles in work	Row count
RC to 000. Cast on 64 sts in MC A in 2 x 1 rib setup			0
K14R of 2 x 1 rib	T4	64	14
Trfr sts to MB onto 66 ndls. RC to 000	T6	66	0
Insert punchcard into machine and lock in start position			
K2R in MC A, K2R in MC C, K2R in MC A	T6	66	6
Note: if using a Brother machine you need to prepare your needles for Fair Isle knitting after R5			
Switch Fair Isle knitting on (see Chapter 1)			
K40R of Fair Isle changing colours every 4R as per the colour chart	T6	66	46
Cancel Fair Isle knitting			
K2R in MC A, K2R in MC C, K2R in MC A	T6	66	52
Change to T5 and K14R in MC A	T5	66	66
Cast off using transfer tool cast off behind the sinker posts		0	

Cowl

Instruction	Tension	Needles in work	Row count
Cast on 96 sts in WY and K10R. Carr at RHS	T5	96	0
Insert punchcard into machine and lock in start position RC to 000			
K8R in MC A, K2R in MC C, K2R in MC A	T5	96	12
Note: if using a Brother machine you need to prepare your needles for Fair Isle knitting after R11			
Switch Fair Isle knitting on (see Chapter 1)			
Section #1 short:			
K40R of Fair Isle changing colours every 4R as per the Colour Chart Section #1 Short	T6	96	52
Cancel Fair Isle knitting and lock card in position			
K2R in MC A, K2R in MC C, K12R in MC A, K2R in MC D, K2R in MC A	T6	96	72
Section #2 long:			
Switch Fair Isle knitting on and set stop knob to Long (L)			
K56R of Fair Isle changing colours every 8R as per the Colour Chart Section #2 Long	T6	96	128
Cancel Fair Isle knitting, re-set stop knob to Short (S) & lock card in position			
K2R in MC A, K2R in MC D, K12R in MC A, K2R in MC B, K2R in MC A	T6	96	148
Switch Fair Isle knitting on			
Section #3 short:			
K40R of Fair Isle changing colours every 4R as per the Colour Chart Section #3 Short	T6	96	188
Cancel Fair Isle knitting and lock card in position			
K2R in MC A, K2R in MC B, K12R in MC A, K2R in MC C, K2R in MC A	T6	96	208
Section #4 long:			
Switch Fair Isle knitting on and set stop knob to Long (L)			
K56R of Fair Isle changing colours every 8R as per the Colour Chart Section #4 Long	T6	96	264
Cancel Fair Isle knitting, re-set stop knob to Short (S) and lock card in position			
K2R in MC A, K2R in MC C, K12R in MC A, K2R in MC D, K2R in MC A	T6	96	284
Switch Fair Isle knitting on			
Section #5 short:			
K40R of Fair Isle changing colours every 4R as per the Colour Chart Section #5 Short	T6	96	324
Cancel Fair Isle knitting and lock card in position			
K2R in MC A, K2R in MC D, K12R in MC A, K2R in MC B, K2R in MC A	T6	96	344
Section #6 long:			
Switch Fair Isle knitting on and set stop knob to Long (L)			
K56R of Fair Isle changing colours every 8R as per the Colour Chart Section #6 Long	T6	96	400
Cancel Fair Isle knitting, re-set stop knob to Short (S) & lock card in position			
K2R in MC A, K2R in MC B, K8R in MC A	T6	96	412
Change to WY and K10R. Cut and remove from machine.			

Making up

See Chapter 3 for details on how to block your knitting. Pin out your cowl and wrist warmers to the measurements given at the start of the pattern.

Wrist warmers

Once dry, fold in half with right sides facing. Using your preferred method, seam along the open edge leaving a 5cm gap for the thumbhole, 8.5cm up from the bottom cuff edge. Take care to match all patterns at the join.

Cowl

Pick up the last row of live stitches at one end of the cowl and hook them back onto the needles with the right side facing you. Push all the stitches to the back of the needles. Fold the cowl up with right sides facing each other and pick up the other row of live stitches. Place these stitches into the hook of the same needles. Working gradually from one end, push the needles back into B position pulling the stitches in the hooks of the needles through the stitches at the back of the needles. Cast off all stitches and remove waste yarn.

Take care to match your patterns at the seam on your wrist warmers.

CHAPTER 3

CORRECTING MISTAKES AND PERFECT FINISHING

The difference between good knitting and great knitting is often down to the finishing. Even the most experienced machine knitters can still make mistakes and sometimes accidents happen. But knowing how to deal with them (and correct them) can help you to achieve perfection in the end.

FIXING COMMON PROBLEMS

The beauty of Fair Isle knitting is that once it is set up and you are knitting away it should be really quick and easy to produce gorgeous coloured knitting. Now that you have started to experiment with more complicated techniques there are many more opportunities for mistakes and accidents to happen and you may even find that you need to rip back some rows and re-do them. Even experienced knitters encounter these same problems. They are just quicker at fixing them. Here are a few problems that are specific to Fair Isle that are good to get to grips with early on.

Picking up dropped stitches

This happens from time to time for a whole host of reasons. Once you spot it, you could try and correct it whilst it's still on the machine but you will be working from the reverse and trying to read back to see which colours you need to pick up depending

You can use a safety pin to hold a dropped stitch.

Once the knitting is off the machine it is much easier to latch the dropped stitch back up from the right side.

where you are on the pattern. I find that by far the easiest and quickest way is to catch the dropped stitch and secure it with a safety pin, stitch marker or a knot of yarn so it doesn't ladder back any further. Then, once the knitting is off the machine, you can work from the correct side of the fabric and use your latch tool to knit back the stitches in the correct colours and use a few stitches on the reverse side to secure it.

Mis-patterning

Again, there are various reasons why this happens and it's not uncommon. But the scale of the problem can vary. If you have just made a small mistake on your punchcard that affects one or two stitches every repeat then this is quite easy to fix with duplicate stitches after your knitting is removed. It also depends when you spot the mis-patterning; Quite often you might not realize until after the knitting has been removed from the machine that there is a mistake.

If, however, you have a major error, then it is far better if you can spot it when the knitting is still on the machine, as duplicate stitching whole rows would be time consuming and impractical. So it pays to be aware of your knitting as you are going along and keep an eye on the reverse of it to check that it looks broadly correct. We will look at each of these instances separately.

Option 1: Pulling back rows when your knitting is still on the machine.

One of the most common examples of mis-patterning occurs when we forget to change colours in a certain place or use the wrong colour altogether. If you realize whilst your knitting is still on the machine, the best remedy is to pull rows back until you get back to before the mistake occurred. Depending on the nature of your pattern you might choose to pull rows back to the very last correct row. Or if you have a row that is an easy one to re-start from (such as a full plain row) you might want to go back as far as that. You may already be familiar with pulling back rows in plain machine knitting but, if not, there are plenty of free videos online that demonstrate this clearly. I have included some details in the Further Resources at the end of the book.

The situation is a little more complicated in Fair Isle knitting than plain knitting as you also need to make sure that your pattern re-starts in the correct position. The important thing is to keep a note of how many rows you are pulling back and where you need to re-start your pattern from. This is when having your row counter on the correct count for your punchcard pays dividends. I find it easiest if you work through it methodically in the following order.

STEP-BY-STEP: PULLING BACK ROWS AND RE-STARTING FAIR ISLE

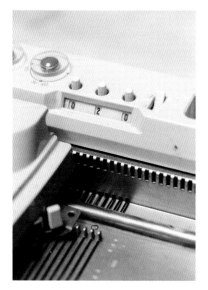

1. Make a note of your row count when you stop.

2. Pull back the knitting by the required number of rows. (It will always need to be an even number of rows so that the yarn ends up on the same side as the carriage.)

3. Turn your row counter back by the relevant number of rows.

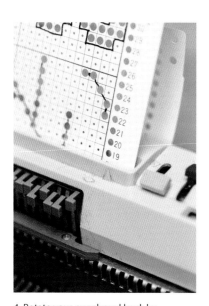

4. Rotate your punchcard back by the same number of rows and lock it in position.

5. IMPORTANT: make sure the carriage has read the correct pattern for the next row before you start knitting again. (We covered this in Chapter 1 if you need to refresh your memory.)

6. Once your carriage is back on the correct side re-thread the yarn into the carriage carefully.

…continued on next page

…continued from previous page

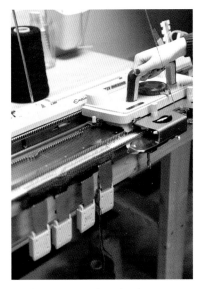

7. Unlock your punchcard and re-start knitting.

Option 2: Picking up dropped knitting and re-starting

Occasionally your Fair Isle knitting will go so wrong that the whole piece drops off your machine or needs to be removed. But this doesn't have to be a total disaster and mean that you have to scrap the entire piece. Depending how many rows you have already knitted it is often worth picking it up and hooking it back onto the machine to re-start. You will have to judge whether you think it is quicker to start again from the beginning or salvage what you already have. It will often depend how far into the piece you were at the time.

If you decide to try and pick it back up, then the easiest way is to try and pull a couple of rows back when it is still off the machine until you get to a row with a very easy pattern repeat to hook back on. If there is one row that is completely one colour then that is ideal but sometimes you also have a 'nice' row that is something like five stitches of colour A, then five stitches of colour B, all the way across.

Once you are back to that row, then use your single-ended transfer tool to start hooking the stitches back onto the needles until they are all back in place. Double-check you haven't dropped or missed any.

All that remains is setting your card and machine up again back in the right position as described in the step-by-step instructions above. Work out which row you hooked back up. Then set your card and row counter to match that. Remember that the actual last row knitted is either five (Silver Reed) or seven (Brother) rows beneath the one you can see on your punchcard reader!

Option 3: Correcting mis-patterning with duplicate stitches

No matter what, no machine is 100 per cent reliable and mis-patterning will happen from time-to-time. Particularly with Fair Isle, it can be hard to spot it sometimes from the reverse of the fabric whilst you are knitting. But that's fine. One of the big benefits of using Shetland-style yarns for Fair Isle knitting is that they are great at disguising things and will bloom after washing to hide what is underneath them. So a duplicate stitch or two can cover any unfortunate errors that occur.

Those are the most common and tricky problems I come across with Fair Isle but you may discover more. It can be frustrating to begin with. But rest assured, the more this happens and the more you practise correcting the mistakes, the more experienced you are becoming as a Fair Isle knitter.

STEP-BY-STEP: DUPLICATE STITCHING TO CORRECT COLOUR

1. Secure the correct colour yarn on the reverse.

2. Bring the needle up at the base of the stitch.

3. Take your needle behind both legs of the stitch above.

4. Insert the needle back in at the base of the stitch.

5. The incorrect stitch has now been covered with the correct colour yarn and once washed it will be invisible.

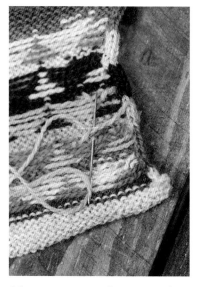

6. Secure your yarn on the reverse and cut.

TECHNIQUES FOR ACHIEVING A PROFESSIONAL FINISH WHILE KNITTING

Mistakes happen for every machine knitter, no matter what their skill level. But what can really elevate your knitting to a professional standard is the care you take in finishing your garment. And this starts whilst your knitting is still on the machine. With Fair Isle knitting, you need to pay particular attention to your floats and colour changes, as you knit, as well as the edges of your knitting. Once your knitting is completed and off the machine you also need to spend time washing and blocking your knitting and joining the seams so that your patterns flow smoothly. After all the knitting, it can sometimes feel such a relief to get it off the machine that you are eager to rush ahead and get the thing finished. But spending the time and attention on the crucial final stages will make a world of difference. I'll explain why in the rest of this chapter.

Dealing with floats

Floats are the lengths of yarn that run along the reverse side of your knitting and they are the tell-tale sign of Fair Isle technique. They can look beautiful in their own right and many knitters take a lot of satisfaction from looking at the reverse of a beautiful Fair Isle garment.

The reverse of a Fair Isle garment can look just as beautiful as the front of the garment.

One quick and easy way to neaten long floats is to hook them up onto a needle on the row above.

But floats can also be problematical. If they are too long, they will look messy and get caught on things like hooks, jewellery and fingers. Because of this, it is considered good design practice to restrict the length of floats to eight stitches or less. We will cover this in more detail in Chapter 5 when we look at designing punchcards. Sometimes, however,

End Needle Selection means that the first needle on any row of Fair Isle knitting is pushed out to D or E position.

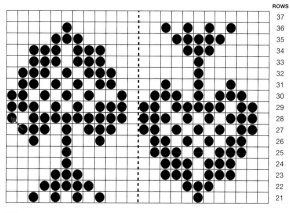

Punch hole/contrast colour

On this pattern the contrast colour stitches on rows 27 and 28 are both near to the edge and row 28 is closer to the edge. The red arrow shows the movement of the contrast yarn between the rows. This means the contrast yarn will move behind the main yarn and close any gaps. It is also easy for the machine to handle.

longer floats can't be avoided in a design. If this is the case, we can still make them workable by hooking them up as we knit. This is another instance when you need to be paying attention as you knit because you need to catch the float before you knit the next row. One helpful tip is to mark up your punchcard with a symbol to look out for on any rows that include a long float. Again, we will cover marking up your punchcards in Chapter 5. Hooking up the float is a very quick and simple technique. All you are doing is using a transfer tool to lift the float and place it in the hook of the needle about half-way along the float. It doesn't have to be precise. Then once you knit the next row, the float will have been caught and knitted in to the reverse of the fabric.

End Needle Selection

I have already mentioned End Needle Selection (ENS) briefly in Chapter 1 because certain Brother models have this as an option on the underneath of the carriage. But it is important for all knitters to understand and use this function when machine knitting Fair Isle.

In its simplest terms, ENS means that the first needle of any row in Fair Isle knitting will always

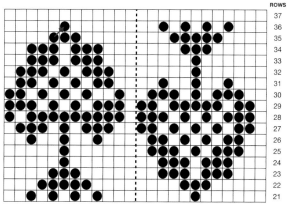

Punch hole/contrast colour

On this pattern, the contrast colour stitches on rows 35 and 36 are both much further from the edge and row 36 is furthest from the edge. The red arrow shows the movement of the contrast yarn between the rows. Without ENA the contrast yarn and main yarn are separated, so you get a gap between the stitches and there is a chance that the contrast yarn will get caught in brushes and mis-knit.

knit the contrast colour, regardless of what the colour should be according to the pattern chart. This can feel wrong at first because sometimes this means that a stitch that should be the main colour is knitted in the contrast colour which will make the pattern incorrect. But, firstly, remember that on most occasions this end stitch will fall within a seam and so not be seen anyway. Perhaps more importantly, ENS helps to solve several other problems that would make your knitting substandard, so it is always worth the compromise.

What difference does ENS make?

In some instances, it will be hard to tell how ENS has made a difference. It all comes down to the design of the pattern and where the final contrast colour stitch falls on two consecutive rows. The following diagrams illustrate when you might encounter problems.

There are three main problems that can occur when you don't use ENS. Firstly, your floats won't always continue all the way to the edge of the knitting. This will mean that you end up with areas around the edge of your knitting that are thinner and flimsier than the rest of the knitting. This can lead to instability and wavy edges that make seaming harder and unattractive.

Secondly, if your contrast yarn moves from an outer position to an inner position over consecutive rows then you will end up with gaps or holes in your knitting where this occurs.

Finally, if you are asking your contrast yarn to make a complicated turn a long way from the edge of the knitting, it is quite likely to get tangled in your brushes or knitting and be knitted into needles and appear as ugly shading on the right side of your knitting.

One of these problems on its own would be enough to ensure you use ENS all the time but the possibility of all three means that it really is vital for perfect Fair Isle knitting.

How to control ENS

As I explained in Chapter 1, later models of Brother machine have a setting underneath the carriage to switch ENS on and off. Check your instruction manual to confirm this and for details of what to do. (If you use DesignaKnit software with your knitting machine you will also have the option to select ENS whatever the make and model of your machine.)

But if you don't have one of these machines, don't worry: you can still operate ENS manually by simply pushing the first needle all the way out to D or E position before you knit every row. It is actually quite a nice repetitive movement that slows you down slightly and allows you to glance at your

On this swatch an identical Fair Isle pattern has been knitted. You can see quite clearly where ENS has been used by the colour of the stitches at the edge of the pink section. This leads to a much neater and more stable edge for seaming.

The reverse of the same swatch. In the pink section ENS was used and on the green section it wasn't. You can see what a difference it makes to the floats on the left-hand edge. You can also see where some of the green yarn has been trapped and knitted into rows where it shouldn't be.

Normally, all these ends would have to be sewn in by hand.

If you have woven the ends in as you knit, then you can simply snip them off once you have washed and blocked your knitting!

knitting before you knit each row. I actually prefer to do it manually rather than automatically.

Be careful about any rows of plain knitting within your Fair Isle pattern. You need to make sure that you don't use ENS for these rows. Otherwise you will end up with a full row-length float all the way across the back of the plain rows. Only use ENS on rows that will contain two colours.

Joining colours and weaving in ends

Weaving in multiple ends of different coloured yarn after the knitting is completed is the bane of many Fair Isle knitters' lives. But by choosing clever ways to join your yarn and weaving in ends as you go, you can eradicate all of that and once your knitting is taken off the machine there is minimal finishing to be done.

This is a technique that will take a bit of practice. You need to make sure that your weaving in is tight enough to get pushed behind the latch of the needle but not too tight that it impedes the needles movement. But don't worry if you don't master it immediately. If you check that the stitch has knitted

cleanly and the loose end has been woven as soon as you have knitted the row, you can unpick it and knit it manually at this stage if there is a problem. It is still far quicker than having to sew in all your ends at the finish.

Placing markers

The final help you can give yourself with knitting a garment is to add stitch markers at key points where you need your garment pieces to match and meet such as at underarm or side neck points. If you are following a published pattern you should be given instructions for when and where to add them (but probably not how!). If you are devising your own pattern it's worthwhile remembering to calculate where you might want to include these. They may seem tiny, trivial additions in the grand scheme of a whole garment but they really make it a lot easier to match up garment pieces when you want to join the seams.

The key thing to remember with stitch markers is that they are different to the markers you add when you knit a tension square. On a tension square you are actually using a contrast yarn to knit a stitch in

1. When you have finished using colour 1, cut the end leaving approximately 10cm (4in).

2. If working from the right-hand edge, take the cut end and weave it clockwise around the needle two to the left.

3. Then continue and weave it clockwise around needle four to the left.

4. Then move back and weave it anti-clockwise around needle three.

5. Secure the loose end under a claw weight and knit one row.

6. Check that the three weaving needles have knitted the yarn through cleanly. If not, unpick the stitch and re-knit it manually.

your swatch and if you removed it afterwards you would have a dropped stitch. For a stitch marker, it is only there to match pieces and then you will want to remove it after you have completed your seams. Therefore it needs to sit on top of your edge stitch (not be a stitch in its own right).

To add a marker, follow the three simple steps below:

1. Take a short piece of yarn (approximately 5cm or 2in) in a contrasting colour and loop it in half.
2. Using your latch tool, go behind (not through) the edge stitch.
3. Place the loop into the hook of your tool. Pull the spare ends of the yarn through the loop and it will be attached around the stitch.

TECHNIQUES FOR ACHIEVING A PROFESSIONAL FINISH AFTER YOU HAVE COMPLETED YOUR KNITTING

Blocking

If you are a hand knitter you may already be familiar with the technique of washing and blocking your knitwear after you have finished knitting. If so, you probably already understand the difference it makes to your finished garment. With Fair Isle knitting it is even more important as it removes the oil and allows the wool to bloom and meld together, creating a warm and stable fabric. It also allows you to make sure that all your patterning is lined up straight and evenly and makes it far easier to complete any seams.

There is a lot of fancy blocking equipment available on the market and whilst this can be a nice upgrade if you knit a lot of garments, don't be fooled into thinking it is necessary. At the most basic level, you probably have almost all the equipment you need already: a towel, some pins and a tape measure.

Blocking Fair Isle knitting transforms it and also makes it much easier to join the final seams.

All you really need to block your knits are a towel, some pins and a tape measure.

Matching patterns at the seams adds a professional look to any finished knitwear.

Using a linker to create seams is an art in its own right.

Blocking is a whole topic in its own right, and one that is worth getting to grips with if you plan to knit lots of garments. There are several resources available online and I have included details at the end of the book.

Joining seams

The final part of completing your knitting project will be to join stitches (or edges) together to finish the seams in your garment. In most instances you have the choice of three methods for seaming: by hand, using your knitting machine, or using a purpose-built linker.

Finishing by hand

This technique is identical to how you would join seams in hand knitting. The fact that you have created the pieces on a knitting machine make little difference. The most common technique is called Mattress Stitch. But any resources for seaming by hand can be followed and I have included details at the back of the book. This can be a very time-consuming method and may well take you longer than machine knitting the entire garment but many people prefer it because it gives you a lot of control over the finish and can be done comfortably on your lap away from the machine.

Finishing using a linker

A linker is a separate piece of equipment that is only used for joining seams on knitwear. It is still used in industry today and not every knitter will have access to one. But if you do, you will have the ability to create seams of chain stitch in the same yarn as that garment that are neat and extremely stretchy. The technique of beautiful linking can be an art in its own right and I have provided details in the Further Resources on this topic.

Finishing on the machine

Whilst having a separate linker can be a nice additional resource for serious machine knitters, it is not a requisite as you can use the knitting machine itself to complete all seams. The method you use will depend on the type of stitches you want to join and the positioning of the seam.

Joining finished edges

In a lot of cases, you will be joining seams that are already finished edges; either they have been cast off already or they are side seams and so the edge of the knitting. In one sense finished edges are easier because you don't have to worry about missing a stitch and creating a ladder. But it's also not always clear exactly what you should be picking

1. Take your first piece and use your transfer tool to hook Piece 1 onto the needles with the right side facing you. Start at each end and work towards the centre point.

2. Try and hook a straight, even channel exactly one stitch in from the edge.

3. Repeat for Piece 2, ensuring right sides are facing each other and you match up any pins or markers.

4. Push both pieces to the back of the needles and add claw weights. Then cast off with a transfer tool cast off.

up and placing on a needle so it calls for more eye judgement.

In this instance, I focus on the desired finished length of the seam and the tension of your seam. I always try to do my final seams once the garment pieces have been blocked so the edges that you are working with should be their final dimension and without any curl. You can then hold these up against the bed of the machine to the length of the final seam. Make sure that you are not stretching the pieces longer than they need to be, or bunching them up or gathering them to get them onto the needles. If you have particularly long seams you can use pins to mark quarter points on each piece so that you know you are matching them evenly.

Joining live seams – stitch to stitch joining

Quite often if you're following a pattern you will be directed to cast off pieces onto waste yarn and this is usually so that when you come to join seams you can use live stitches rather than a cast off edge and you will achieve a much better finish, not having to worry about the stretchiness of your seam. With live stitches you need to be really careful that every stitch ends up on a needle and is cast off before you remove the waste yarn – otherwise you will have dropped stitches and ladders.

You follow the same steps as above for joining finished edges except that now you are picking up the last live stitch before you changed to waste yarn. You can check that you have done this correctly when you get to the end as you will know how many stitches you finished with on the final row and you can make sure this is the same as the number of needles you have filled.

Once Piece 1 has been hooked up with the right side facing you, you push it all the way to the back of the needles. Then repeat for Piece 2 but make sure that the stitches stay in the hook of the needle.

Complete the seam by pulling the needles back gradually to B position, working evenly from one end all the way along and this will pull the stitches

A shoulder seam is normally a perfect opportunity to join live seams that can give an almost invisible finish.

from Piece 2 through Piece 1 and you will end up with one set of stitches on the needles and the other stitches will have been knitted off. You can then cast off as before.

I love using this technique as it is really accurate, pretty quick to complete and can often look almost invisible from the front of the garment. If you are a hand knitter it is very similar, in method and effect, to a three needle bind off.

Joining mixed seams

You might also have a seam that is a combination of both of these – so one edge might be a finished edge but the trim you want to join to it (for example) might be on waste yarn. In this instance you use the method for finished edges on the first piece and push this to the back of the needles. You then add the live stitches from the trim into the hooks of the needle and carry on exactly as you would do for joining live seams above.

STEP-BY-STEP: JOINING MIXED SEAMS

1. Hook Piece 1 with the finished edge onto the machine with the right side facing you.

2. Push Piece 1 to the back of the needles and hook the live stitches from Piece 2 into the hook of the needles with right sides facing each other.

3. Gradually push back all the needles so that the latches close over Piece 2 and pull those stitches through Piece 1. You now only have stitches from Piece 2 on the needles and you can add weights and cast off.

Now that we have covered correcting any mistakes and techniques for professional finishing, you can apply everything we have learnt so far in the following pattern for a cushion cover.

PROJECT 3: NORTHERN WAVES PATTERNED CUSHION COVER

The pattern for this cushion cover is a progression from the cowl and wrist warmers in Chapter 2 and will test a lot of the finishing skills we discussed in this chapter such as weaving in ends, adding markers, and using End Needle Selection.

You still don't need to worry about shaping yet, but blocking will be important to end up with a perfect rectangle for easy seaming. This design uses a punchcard I have designed so you will need to punch this yourself. You can read how to do this in Chapter 5 or simply choose one of the pre-punched cards that you already have and choose your own colour layout.

Yarn

- Northern Yarn 'Methera' Cheviot/BFL/Shetland/ Zwartbles 100% British Wool 4 ply
- 100g in each colour (400g total)
  - Col A = Teal
  - Col B = Ginger
  - Col C = Raspberry
  - Col D = Natural Grey

This will give you enough yarn for two cushion covers as well as adequate yarn for practice swatches and tension squares.

The rib envelope closure on the cushion cover helps to give a lovely, neat finish.

The geometric pattern gives this cushion cover a Scandi feel.

Knitting machine

Knitted on a standard-gauge Knitmaster 360.

Punchcard Pattern Chart

The pattern is worked using the Northern Waves punchcard and uses four colours for the patterning. (See Appendix at the back of the book for copies of all the punchcards used.)

Tension

- 28 sts and 32 rows to 10cm (4in) in Fair Isle pattern. Tension dial at T9.1.

Size and finished measurements

- One size
- Cushion cover: 30cm (11¾ in) wide x 18.5cm (45¼ in) long when folded.
- This fits a 31 x 46cm (12¼ x 18¼ in) cushion pad. If you want to use a different size cushion pad, adjust your number of stitches and rows accordingly.

Colour charts

See Appendix at the back of the book.

Pattern instructions

Cushion cover

The pattern below is written to include a rib cuff at the start. If you do not have a ribber attachment, then you can use a mock rib on your main bed instead.

Making up

See earlier in this chapter for details on how to block your knitting. Pin out your cushion cover to the measurements given at the start of the pattern.

Once dry, lay your knitting flat with right side up. Use the diagram above to fold into shape. Fold piece one along the fold line between the markers at Row 90 with right sides facing each other. Repeat along the fold between markers at Row 234. Using your preferred method, seam along each edge. This may be reasonably bulky as you will have three edges in the seam in some places. Fold right sides out and fill with your cushion pad.

Instruction	Tension	Needles in work	Row count
RC to 000. Cast on 84 sts in MC A in 2x2 rib setup			0
Insert punchcard into machine and lock in start position			
K12R of 2x2 rib in MC A	T6	84	12
Trfr sts to MB onto 84 ndls. RC to 000	T6	84	0
Switch Fair Isle knitting on (see Chapter 1 if you need a reminder how to do this)			
K90R of Fair Isle changing colours every 4R as per the colour chart. Pay close attention to switching the colour from Yarn Feeder A/1 to Yarn Feeder B/2 every 6R (see colour chart for details)	T9.1	84	90
Add stitch markers at both edges on RC 90	T9.1	84	90
Continue knitting in Fair Isle pattern and add more stitch markers at both edges on RC 234	T9.1	84	234
Continue knitting in Fair Isle pattern until RC 368	T9.1	84	368
Cancel Fair Isle knitting			
Cast off using transfer tool cast off behind the sinker posts			0

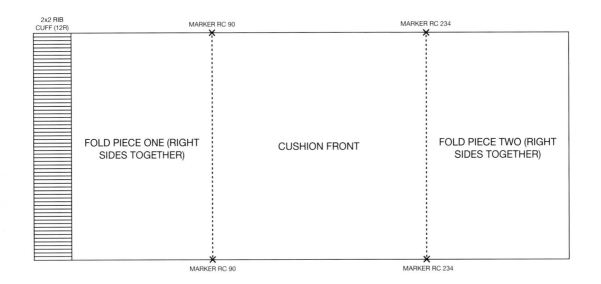

Northern Waves cushion construction.

The cushion cover folds in a pillow slip construction.

Keep all your swatches labelled and neatly organised and you have a library of resources for future projects.

Weaving in your ends as you knit means you can simply snip them all off at the end, saving the need for laboriously sewing them in.

CHAPTER 4

HOW TO COMBINE FAIR ISLE INTO ANY PART OF YOUR KNITTING

B y this stage you should be getting nice and familiar with your machine and your punch-cards and be confident enough to knit full swatches of patterns in various colours and yarns. And this is great – as long as you only ever want to knit scarves or cushion covers or anything else that requires an all-over pattern with no shaping what-soever. But you will probably grow tired of this quite quickly and want to expand your repertoire further so that you can incorporate Fair Isle into full gar-ments and choose how and where it is positioned. That is what we will be looking at in this chapter.

Once you have knitted a lot of cushion covers you may be keen to try some new shapes.

POSITIONING YOUR FAIR ISLE PATTERNS

Moving your Fair Isle pattern horizontally

The techniques that you have practised in the pre-vious chapters all dealt with all over full patterning and because it was mainly swatches it didn't matter exactly where the pattern repeats fell. But there are many occasions when you will want to dictate exactly how the pattern lies on the piece of knitting. The most common example is when you are knitting jumpers and cardigans and you want the design to be repeated from the centre out. This is particularly desirable if your Fair Isle pattern is geometric in design or has a very obvious vertical repeat.

Equally, there may be times where moving the pattern placement left or right will give a more pleasing and flattering design. For example, this can be a consideration when you have larger motifs that may land on the bust area.

Earlier in the book, we covered how to start and finish your punchcard so that your pattern knits correctly in the vertical direction. In effect, you are simply switching between sections of Fair Isle knit-ting and plain knitting. Now we need to understand how to plan your punchcard knitting so that you control the horizontal placement of the pattern and remedy the sort of problems described above. The good news is that it is relatively straightforward and the machines have some helpful ways of assisting you.

On this cardigan the pattern has been allowed to knit randomly exactly where it falls on the needle bed and it looks very unbalanced.

On this second cardigan, however, the knitter has taken time to either design the punchcard, or knit on a specific area of the bed, such that the vertical pattern lines are balanced equally from the centre front of the cardigan.

This pattern layout would be considered unfortunate because of where the large flowers appear.

By nudging the pattern horizontally, the pattern layout is much more acceptable.

How to work out where the pattern repeat will fall

As you know, when set to knit, the machine will repeat the punchcard pattern every 24 stitches (or 12 or 36) across the entire width and it does this from centre needle 0 outwards. So for example on a standard gauge machine, one full repeat will be placed between left needle 12 and right needle 12 and then it will repeat from there until it runs out of cast on needles. So whatever runs down the centre of your punchcard will also run down the centre of your knitting if you always cast on centrally across your needle bed. If you want to change this you either need to design your punchcard with a different centre line or move the position of your knitting on the machine. To make it easier for you to visualize, your needle bed number strip will be marked with diamonds and crosses (Silver Reed) or red horizontal lines and bows (Brother) that correspond with the markings on your punchcard reader.

The easiest way to understand this is to try it out yourself and knit swatches from one of your pre-punched cards but with different positioning.

How to set off knitting so the pattern is placed correctly

Whenever you are planning to knit a garment with a Fair Isle pattern you want to consider this before you start knitting so you can be confident that the pattern will fall pleasingly. If the shapes in the pattern are quite small and repetitive (such as polka dots), it probably won't cause any issues however the pattern falls. But many Fair Isle designs will have obvious vertical lines or centre points that will be very visible especially when worn on the body and viewed from a distance. It might take you a bit of time to check the layout, but it will be worth it for a finished garment that looks just right.

A Silver Reed machine will repeat the punchcard pattern between every cross.

On a Brother machine the pattern repeats across the solid red bars between each solid bow.

Here the top swatch is knitted over 72 stitches centred on the needle bed (left needle 36 to right needle 36). Whilst the bottom swatch is still knitted over 72 stitches but they have been cast on in a different position on the needle bed between left needle 48 and right needle 24.

I find that the easiest way to check your layout is to quickly draw a rough sketch of your pattern pieces and scribble on any vertical lines or large motifs. These sketches don't need to be works of art and they don't have to be entirely accurate or to scale; they are a quick way to see if you need to amend your design or move your knitting on the bed. The places to pay particular attention to are the centre front of the garment, around the neckline, and perhaps down the centre line of the sleeves and any points where patterns might meet each other at seams. If you are happy that the pattern falls exactly as you want it, when centred on the machine, then you don't need to do anything.

If, however, you do want to shift your pattern or knitting you have two choices: you can re-punch your card so that the design moves left or right on it; or you can move your knitting on the bed and use the original punchcard. The second option saves you having to re-design or re-punch your card, but if you are then following a knitting pattern you will need to remember to allow for your moves whenever there is any shaping indicated.

Option 1: Adapting the punchcard
You will need to decide how far you need to move your pattern to centre it. If you need to shift the pattern by twelve places either way, you would take the pattern on one half of the punchcard and move it adjacent to the pattern on the other side. You might find that sketching this out on graph paper helps you to visualize it more easily before you mark up your punchcard.

Whilst this might feel like a lot of extra work, once you have amended your punchcard you can follow your garment pattern instructions exactly and cast on your knitting based on the original needle bed layout.

Option 2: Moving your knitting on the needle bed
If you decide to keep your original punchcard but you want to move the positioning of your knitting,

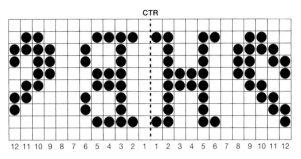

Punch hole

The original pattern needs to shift by twelve places either way so that the heart motif falls in the centre.

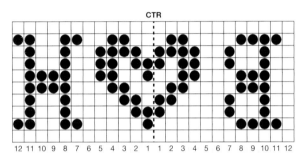

Punch hole

I have now shifted my pattern by twelve stitches and everything is centred pleasingly.

then you will need to cast on in a different needle position on the machine and it will no longer be centred on the bed. This can become confusing once you get to areas of shaping, such as armholes, as your needle numbering will be different on the left and right and so it will be harder to follow your knitting pattern.

Which of the two options you choose will depend on the complexity and length of the punchcard involved and the shaping of the garment. If I were knitting a scarf or snood with a punchcard of over 100 rows then I would move my knitting off-centre. However, if my punchcard pattern was only 50–70 rows and I was knitting a set-in sleeve jumper with a V neck, I would punch a new card for that design so that I could follow the pattern accurately for all the shaping required.

Using Fair Isle in borders or sections

With many designs you won't want to use your Fair Isle pattern across the entire garment. Often you might only want to add a border of it at the cuffs or hem, or perhaps a panel down the centre front of a garment. This is quite easy to do but it will differ depending on whether you want a horizontal border or a vertical panel.

Horizontal sections of Fair Isle

This is very straightforward and is a case of switching between plain knitting and Fair Isle knitting (and then back again) wherever you want a border to appear. This is what we covered in Chapter 2 and is also the technique used for the cowl and wrist warmers pattern at the end of that chapter. So, for example, if you wanted a border that was 20 rows of a particular pattern and you wanted it to be placed 10 rows above the top of the hem you would follow the sequence below.

- Set up your punchcard and lock it in position.
- Knit 10 rows of plain knitting (if you are using a Brother machine make sure you have selected your needles after row 9).
- Switch to Fair Isle knitting and knit 20 rows of the punchcard with two colours.
- Turn off Fair Isle knitting and return to plain knitting for the rest of your garment.

It really is as simple as that. The main things that you need to remember are to make sure your punchcard is locked in the correct position so the design starts where you want it to (remember that difference of 5 or 7 rows that we discussed in Chapter 1) and that you remember to switch your carriage back to plain knitting as soon as you want your pattern to end (otherwise you will drop stitches or all of your knitting).

Vertical panels of Fair Isle (single motif knitting)

Knitting a vertical panel is a little bit more complicated and you will need to use some additional parts from your toolbox to set the machine up for this. You might have been wondering why you had what looked like small pieces of lego in your toolbox; now you will get a chance to use them.

You will need all of these accessories for motif knitting on a Silver Reed machine.

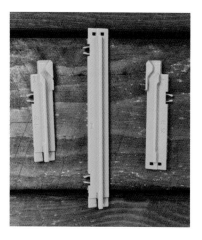

You will need to use (some or all of) the motif knitting cams from your toolbox with a Brother machine.

In your instruction manual this technique will probably be referred to as 'Single Motif Knitting' which can be confusing and lead you to overlook the function. Single motif refers to the technique in which you want to knit one distinct shape, such as a teddy bear or a cat, in a particular position in your knitting. It is like a small-scale intarsia pattern but with the limitation of two colours. For this reason, I find single motif in the true sense to be quite limited

Weaving in ends of main yarn at the edge of your panels as you knit avoids unsightly gaps. Here I have deliberately used a contrast colour yarn to highlight the position.

Motif knitting can be a really effective way of adding vertical patterned panels to your knitting.

If you don't weave in an extra end then you end up with a gap in your knitting between the two sections.

in its uses. However, this technique is extremely useful if you want to knit vertical sections of patterned Fair Isle.

You will need to follow the set-up instructions for your particular model of machine because it will vary but the basic principle is to add the relevant cams to your needle bed before you start. (On Brother machines you will also have to turn your Change Knob to 'SM' whenever you want to knit single motif.) After that you operate your machine in the normal way for Fair Isle knitting but instead of the pattern being knitted across the whole width of your knitting, it will only appear between the cams. All the same principles apply, such as picking up the patterning the row before you start.

Avoiding yarn separation at the edge of your Fair Isle panel

When you have a mixture of vertical areas of plain knitting and Fair Isle knitting you will get variations in the thickness of the fabric; the plain section will be thinner because it won't have floats running across the back. This is something you need to consider before using this technique. But often this can elevate a design because there will be variety between each of the panels. What you want to avoid, though, is having unsightly gaps where the knitting switches between the two areas.

To do this you will need to weave in ends of the main colour yarn onto the needles at the edge of the motif knitting panel on the carriage side of the knitting. This will vary slightly depending on your machine, so refer to your instruction manual.

USING FAIR ISLE IN GARMENTS WITH SHAPING

So far all of the knitting we have done has been with straight edges and there has been no need for shaping at all. But there are plenty of times when you will want to shape seams or edges on a garment that is knitted in Fair Isle. The most common occasions will be armhole and neckline shaping. Many knitters worry that they don't know how to deal with these instances without creating a mess. But as long as you have followed and understood everything we have covered so far, you should be more than ready to give this a go. The pattern at the end of this chapter is for a shaped pom-pom hat and will give you an opportunity to practise the following techniques.

Shaping at edges of rows – fully fashioned shaping

Depending on your current level of machine knitting experience, you might already be competent at shaping on plain stocking stitch. Fair Isle knitting really isn't any different. You just need to be mindful of the fact that you will have floats on the back of the knitting and what effect moving stitches will have on the patterning. There are several ways of increasing and decreasing stitches for shaping. But the most professional finish you can use is 'fully fashioned shaping' whereby you move a certain number of stitches in or out to either decrease or increase and that is what we will cover here.

Fully fashioned shaping adds a professional look to the edges of your knitting.

By using fully fashioned shaping you create a visible edge channel on the right side of your knitwear. This has a pleasing and professional look to it. Standard instructions will tell you to use your three-ended transfer tool to move your stitches and this will create the increase or decrease on the third needle from the edge. If you have a multi-ended transfer tool, you have the option to move up to seven stitches from the edge. Whatever number of stitches you choose, this will define the width of your visible channel and is often a case of personal preference. In the examples below I have just used a standard three-ended tool.

STEP-BY-STEP: FULLY FASHIONED DECREASES

Can be worked on both ends or either end.

1. Use your three-ended transfer tool to pick up the last three edge stitches.

2. Move the stitches one position further *in* and tip them onto those needles.

3. You will now have two stitches on the third needle from the edge. Continue knitting.

STEP-BY-STEP: FULLY FASHIONED INCREASES

Can be worked on both ends or either end.

1. Use your three-ended transfer tool to pick up the last three edge stitches.

2. Move the stitches one position further *out* and tip them onto those needles. You will now have an empty needle on the fourth needle from the edge.

3. Using your transfer tool, pick up the heel of the adjacent stitch.

4. Place the heel onto the empty needle. Continue knitting.

Shaping in the centre of a row – partial knitting

The other time when you will really need to pay attention to the shaping in relation to your Fair Isle patterning is when you are using Hold position to only knit on certain sections of the needle bed at any one time. This is known as 'partial knitting' and is the standard way to knit necklines.

Controlling which needles will knit and which needles will hold

Combining Fair Isle patterning with hold position can cause many knitters a headache. I find that it really helps if you understand what you are asking the machine to do in terms of needle positions.

When you set up partial knitting you will choose which needles you want to continue knitting and which needles will hold the existing stitches. Once you have selected 'Hold' on your machine any needles in B position will continue to select and knit as before whenever the carriage passes over them. Any needles in D or E position will hold the stitch and do nothing.

The table below highlights what will happen in each needle position when your carriage is set to Hold and you are knitting Fair Isle.

By pushing certain needles all the way out to D or E position and using the Hold function you can choose to knit only on part of the needle bed (partial knitting).

Needle position	What the machine will do
A	Does not knit
B	Knits Fair Isle pattern – main colour
C (Silver Reed) or D (Brother)	Knits Fair Isle pattern – contrast colour
D (Silver Reed) or E (Brother)	Holds the previous stitches – does not knit

Your punchcard will control moving needles between B and C/D position automatically. You will control moving needles between 'Hold' and 'not Hold'. The reason this is important is so that you understand what will happen when you push needles into hold and also when you re-introduce them into work.

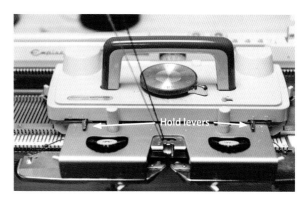

Use the Russell levers on both sides to set the Silver Reed carriage to hold. '|' = Hold.

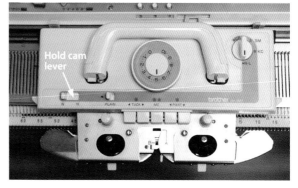

On a Brother carriage the Holding Cam Lever switch controls the hold function. H = Hold.

If you are using End Needle Selection (ENS) for your knitting you will need to bear this in mind as well. If your machine is performing ENS automatically for you, then you don't need to worry. But if you are manually pushing your end needle to D or E position for ENS, you will need to change this and only push it out to C or D instead, otherwise your end needle won't knit.

How to re-start your pattern in the correct place on a garment

If you are using partial knitting to shape a neckline on a garment, you will knit the body as far as the start of the neck shaping. At this point, you will put one half of the needles into hold whilst you knit the garment on one side of the neck only. Once that is complete you will then move back to the other side of the neck and repeat the process. The skill here is to make sure that your patterns are identical on either side. We will practise this technique fully in the hat pattern at the end of this chapter and also in the vest pattern later in the book.

When you get to the section in a pattern where you need to divide your knitting and knit on one side only, the most important thing to remember is to make a note of the row of your punchcard you are about to knit. Once you have noted this down somewhere, you can continue following the instructions and complete that side of the garment.

Then when you are ready to knit the other half of the garment you need to move your punchcard back to the same position again and lock it in position. You can then pick up the pattern as described in Chapter 1 (by running the carriage past the card reader with no yarn in the carriage and the carriage out of work). If you are using a Brother machine the selected needles will have moved into position before you start so you can check that they match

It is vital to make a note of the row number when you stop your punchcard. In this instance Row 33 will be the next row to be knitted. But remember, this isn't the same as the row of patterning that is visible on your punchcard reader (it is 5 or 7 rows below).

the pattern on the other side. If you are using Silver Reed you won't be able to see this and so you will need to be confident that you have followed this step correctly.

Once you have picked up the correct row of the pattern, you can set your machine back up for Fair Isle knitting and continue following the pattern instructions. Remember to make sure you have moved your row counter back as well to coincide with the pattern instructions.

Practice makes perfect!

This is quite a tricky process to explain succinctly and the easiest way to understand it is to put it into practice. The following pattern for the hat will help you do just that. To knit this hat you will knit across all of the needles until you divide to knit the left and right in two separate sections with shaping on each side of the sections, giving you the opportunity to practise everything we have discussed in this chapter.

The design for the Uist Hat highlights the colour differences in the natural shades of yarn.

Katie is wearing a size S hat.

You should now be ready to add some shaped Fair Isle knitting to your repertoire and this hat pattern uses both fully fashioned shaping at the crown as well as holding position to knit the crown in two sections. You will be able to put all the techniques that you have learnt in this chapter into practice.

This design uses a punchcard I have designed based on the mill in North Uist, Scotland, where the yarn is produced. You will need to punch this card yourself and instructions for doing this are given in Chapter 5. Or simply choose one of the pre-punched cards that you already have and practise with that first of all.

Yarn

- Uist Wool 'Astair' 100% British Alpaca/Wool 4 ply
- 50g in each colour (200g total)
  - Col A = bealach
  - Col B = maol
  - Col C = abhainn
  - Col D = poll
- This will give you enough yarn for two hats as well as adequate yarn for practice swatches and tension squares.

Knitting machine

Knitted on a standard gauge Knitmaster 360.

Punchcard pattern chart

The pattern is worked using the Uist hat punchcard and uses four colours for the patterning. (See the Appendix at the back of the book for copies of all the punchcards used.)

Tension

- 26 sts and 36 rows to 10cm (4in) in Fair Isle pattern. Tension dial at T10.1.

Size and finished measurements

- Sizes: Small, Medium, Large
- Finished circumference: 46cm (18¼ in), 55cm (21½ in), 64cm (25¼ in)
- Length from crown: 21cm (8¼ in)
- Pom pom circumference: 8cm (3¼ in)

Colour charts

See the Appendix at the back of the book.

Pattern instructions

Hat

The pattern below is written to include a rib cuff at the start. If you do not have a ribber attachment, then you can use a mock rib on your main bed instead.

Instruction	Tension	Needles in work	Row count
RC to 000. Cast on 122 (146, 170) sts in MC A in 2x2 rib setup	T0	122 (146, 170)	0
Insert punchcard into machine and lock in start position			
K16R of 2x2 rib in total (4R in MC B, 4R in MC C, 4R in MC D)	T6	122 (146, 170)	16
Trfr sts to MB onto 122 (145, 170) ndls. RC to 000	T10.1	122 (146, 170)	0
Switch Fair Isle knitting on (see Chapter 1 if you need a reminder how to do this)			
K36R of Fair Isle changing colours as per the colour chart. Finish with COR	T10.1	122 (146, 170)	36
Start crown shaping RHS			
Push 61 (73, 85) ndls on LHS into Hold position. Switch carriage to Hold	T10.1	61 (73, 85)	36
Continue knitting in Fair Isle pattern on RHS ndls only and K 1R	T10.1	61 (73, 85)	37
Dec 1st f/f each side and every foll alt row until RC 60	T10.1	37 (49, 61)	60
Break yarns leaving a long tail on one of them and sew this back through all of the stitches in work on RHS. Remove these stitches from the machine.			
Move to COL and cancel Hold. Put all ndls on LHS back into work.		61 (73, 85)	
Turn punchcard back to R 36 and RC to 036. Pick up Fair Isle patterning on the needles.			36
Start crown shaping LHS			
Continue knitting in Fair Isle pattern on LHS ndls and K 1R	T10.1	61 (73, 85)	37
Dec 1st f/f each side and every foll alt row until RC 60	T10.1	37 (49, 61)	60
Cancel Fair Isle knitting	T10.1	37 (49, 61)	60
Break yarns leaving a long tail on one of them and sew this back through all of the stitches in work on RHS. Remove remaining stitches from the machine.			

Making up

See Chapter 3 for details on how to block your knitting. Pin out your hat to the measurements given at the start of the pattern.

Once dry, fold your hat in half and using your preferred method, seam along both edges.

Pom-pom

Use a pom-pom maker to make the pom-pom using a mixture of all four colours. Using the long yarn end at the top of each crown half, gather the knitting and stitch it tightly in the centre. Attach the pom-pom securely.

The pom-pom is entirely optional but looks effective with a mixture of all four colours.

CHAPTER 5

DESIGNING YOUR OWN PUNCHCARDS

Now we are ready to move into my favourite part of Fair Isle knitting, which is designing your own patterns. When machine knitters have mastered the basics of Fair Isle punchcard knitting, they are often keen to develop their own unique designs but they may feel unsure of how to proceed or become frustrated when the ideas in their head don't translate to successful designs. This section will take away the mystery and introduce you to the process.

For me this is the part when Fair Isle truly becomes a magical tool – when you can literally create any pattern you like and play around and develop it in swatches. My original pattern for 'Hebden Houses' developed in exactly that way. I took a class in machine quilting for fun and we used a design for Hebden Bridge. Once I was home I was interested to explore how it would translate into machine knitting and the rest, as they say, is history.

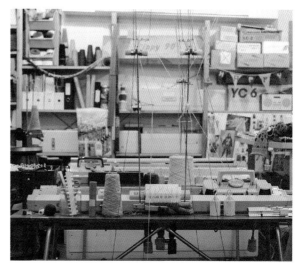

My original quilt panel was the inspiration for my 'Hebden Houses' Fair Isle pattern.

CREATING YOUR OWN DESIGNS – DESIGN PRINCIPLES

Finding inspiration and translating it into punchcard designs

I've already shared where I got the original inspiration for one of my designs and I have a number of 'go-to' places that always leave me bursting with ideas: museum trips, artwork, books and magazines, other craft disciplines (I love looking at quilting and graphic design), and photos from travel and city visits. You will probably already have favourite places of your own. If you are struggling to think of anything, consider what images make you smile or happy when you look at them. They really can be absolutely anything, from a packet of food to a bunch of flowers on your desk.

The main thing to consider when you are designing specifically for Fair Isle is that you are looking for quite small-scale patterns. Remember your design will need to fit into a certain number of stitch repeats and even if you have electronic patterning that allows up to 200 stitches you will still have to consider the length of the floats on the reverse of your knitting. We will discuss these considerations in more detail below but often for larger-scale images intarsia will be a more suitable technique than Fair Isle. Fair Isle is largely meant for 'small' repeating patterns. But this aspect of it is one of the things that I find really calming, in much the same way that colouring books can be.

The 'official' charting paper has a 24-stitch pattern repeat marked on it.

Sketching patterns

Once you have some source material for your new design you are ready to start sketching. It's not strictly necessary to have some inspiration material to sketch from but I find that this is far easier than just trying to come up with a design from your head. Particularly if you haven't designed punchcards before, you can almost 'warm up' by trying to copy exactly what you see in front of you on your inspiration material without any judgement. And then, once you get into the flow, you can start adapting and changing it. The main thing to remember is that there really is no right or wrong way with this; just enjoy yourself by filling in squares on graph paper.

Materials

Which leads me nicely into what materials you need for this. I always start with squared paper and a pencil. If you have ever bought or inherited packs of blank punchcards you should have also received the squared paper that comes with them that will be marked with the stitches and rows with a box showing the full pattern repeat area in it. This is nice to have but not obligatory – any squared paper will do at this stage. And I should also add that even if I am going to be using digital software for my final design, I still tend to start on squared paper first as I love the process of pencil on paper.

I tend to start without any colour and then add colour on later versions. But if you want to add colour to your designs then you will just need some coloured pencils, pens or ink. Recently I had a lovely

Colouring in designs can be a very enjoyable task in its own right.

relaxing hour painting colours onto my chart and I can highly recommend it.

Although regular graph paper is perfectly adequate for designing your patterns, it won't accurately represent the finished shapes of your patterns. This is because the squares in squared paper are exactly square in shape, as opposed to real stitches which are normally wider than their height (which is why you have a different gauge for your stitches and rows). This doesn't affect your design too drastically if you are just trying to gauge the general look and layout of the pattern. But if you are trying to work out exact needles to create a certain shape, such as a circle for example, regular squared paper won't be accurate enough to help you decide exactly where your pattern shaping should be. There are several tools online that are available for printing your own graph paper that mimics the exact dimensions of your stitches and I have included details of these in the Further Resources section.

PUNCHCARD LIMITATIONS AND TECHNICAL CONSIDERATIONS

The creative side of designing repeat patterns can be wonderful but there are certain limitations that you have to consider in order to turn your design into a successful repeating pattern. This is what can often trip up knitters who are trying out their own designs for the very first time. Below are some of the most important things you need to consider.

Pattern repeats

Once you are ready to start sketching, the biggest consideration you need to bear in mind is your pattern repeat. Depending on which machine you will be using this will vary but the most common repeat is 24 stitches wide. If this is the case you will need to make sure that your design fits within this. But also consider how it will repeat either side of it – and also above and below! The official paper that comes with your blank punchcards allows you to do that by extending your repeat in each direction to check that it works.

Even though your full repeat may be 24 stitches you can use smaller repeats within that. A 24-stitch repeat is particularly useful as you can work with combinations of 3, 4, 6, 8, and 12 stitches. This becomes really useful if you move onto patterns that involve decreasing the number of stitches (such as in Fair Isle yokes). We will cover this further in Chapter 6.

Sometimes having to work within boundaries can feel quite restrictive and limiting but artistic theory actually says that it can be one of the greatest tools for creativity. As I mentioned before, if you are using electronic patterning, you don't have such limitations and can work to any number of stitches in one single repeat. Remember though that if you ever want to go back and use that pattern on a standard punchcard machine, it will only work if it fits within the stitch width for that machine; if you ever intend to share your patterns with others and want it to be used on all machines you will still need to pay attention to this.

In this design the shape on the far right will match the shape on the far left when they repeat next to each other; the same applies to top and bottom. The repeat itself is only 12 stitches wide.

Floats

This will be the other major consideration for your design work. A float is the long thread of yarn that is created on the reverse of Fair Isle knitting when the yarn not in use is carried across. Generally it is considered good practice to restrict this to a maximum of eight stitches wide. Once floats get longer than this, they can catch and snag and, depending on where they appear on a garment, can cause problems getting caught on fingers and jewellery.

However, as with most things, there are no hard and fast rules. The easiest solution is to always add patterns into your design to break up any areas of long floats. Small one-stitch 'lice' stitches can be an easy way to do this. In my 'Hebden Houses'

pattern, I added birds between the chimney stacks at the top for this reason. But sometimes this will compromise the look of the design and you have to live with longer floats. In Chapter 3, we looked at methods to knit these in to ease the problem. In the end you have to decide which is the best compromise for your design. Whatever you decide, floats should always be a consideration when charting your pattern.

Digital patterning vs. analogue for designing

I started off designing before I had electronic machines and so I feel very comfortable with designing patterns using pencil and paper and I still prefer to start that way. But if you have a machine that uses electronic patterning you might find it more efficient to start by designing directly into the software. Even if you don't have an electronic machine, there are several sources of software available that will let you chart knitting patterns quite easily and they can be used for charting hand knitting patterns too. The main advantage to using these is the ease and speed you can make amendments and try out different options. I have included details of patterning software in the Further Resources section. The choice will be a personal one but I always start by hand and move to digital at a later stage. I have too much fun drawing and colouring in!

This is a great Fair Isle pattern because all the floats are short and even.

PUNCHING YOUR OWN DESIGNS – PUNCHCARDS

Equipment

- Blank punchcards in the correct stitch number for your machine, i.e. 24 holes (either packs of cards or a continuous roll)
- Hole punch
- Permanent marker pen (or other pen/pencil)
- Tape
- Scissors

You don't need much equipment to punch your own cards. The most important tool is the hole punch.

Once you have designed your new pattern you are ready to physically punch it onto a card so that you can start testing it on swatches. This is a relatively straightforward process but depending on the size of your pattern (the number of rows) it might take you a while. If your pattern is less than 50 rows you will need to punch two full repeats of the pattern so that you have enough length in your card to be able to bend it round to clip into a continuous loop. Unless, that is, you are only ever going to knit a single repeat of it in which case it won't need to be clipped together.

Start by taking your blank card. This might already be pre-cut to a certain length for you – often between 60 and 65 rows long. These cards work for most designs, but I prefer to use the continuous rolls so that I can cut them to the exact length I need. My 'Hebden Houses' pattern is 73 rows long which would be just too long for standard blank punchcards and so I would have to continue onto a second card and clip them together which could cause a few issues over time.

Marking your pattern

The first stage of the process is to mark your pattern onto the punchcard. If you are using official sets of blanks you will normally have the advantage that numbers have already been printed up the side and the top and bottom header rows have already been punched. If you are using a blank roll (like I do) then you will need to also add the two full rows top and bottom as well as the holes for your clips.

This is a 24-stitch, 62-row blank punchcard for a Knitmaster machine. The two rows of holes at the top and the bottom allow for the pattern to continue when you clip your card together and the two holes at either side are where your clips will be positioned.

Here you can see that Row 1 on the right isn't right next to the first row to be punched. It is 5 rows higher because it is a Knitmaster card. Make sure that you mark your pattern starting on the very first available row (which has no number next to it in this example).

Punch the holes by guiding the raised point into the centre of the hole until it slots into position. Then punch your hole.

Start by taking a pen and marking up the holes you want to punch with a permanent marker. You can use any pen but I find non-permanent pens or pencils smudge as you are moving up the card and make a confusing mess. I also label my card at the end with as many useful instructions as possible and I use a permanent marker for that too. The most important thing to remember at this stage is the 5 (Silver Reed) or 7 (Brother) row differential that I explained in Chapter 1.

Punching your pattern

Once all your holes are marked you can start punching. Your hole punch will only reach halfway across the card so you will need to punch all the holes on the right from the right-hand side and then switch to the left for the remaining holes. There is a bit of a knack to punching that you will pick up with practice. Your hole punch will have a very small, raised point in the centre and you want to position this in the tiny hole that already exists. Once you feel it slot into position you can then press the puncher to cut the full hole. Take your time because whilst misalignment and mistakes can be corrected (see below) they increase your chances of mis-patterning especially if you use the same card a lot. If your pattern is particularly long you might want to approach it in stages and just punch a few sets of rows per day.

Correcting mistakes and damage

Mistakes happen and, even if they don't, your cards may still get worn over time and need some repair. All you need for this is some tape. Magic tape, sellotape or masking tape all work. Cut two small pieces the same size as each other and stick this on the front and reverse over the area with the mistake on it. You can then correct your mistake. If your mistake was that you punched a hole where there shouldn't be one then as long as that hole is now covered by tape it will be corrected. Just make sure that your tape doesn't cover up any other holes that should still be holes. If it does just re-punch that hole through the tape. If your mistake was a wonky or misaligned hole, repeat the same process and then re-punch your hole in the correct position. You will need to keep an eye on any cards with tape on them as the tape will start to peel over time and might need to be replaced.

Once your card is punched and all marked up you are ready to use it exactly as you have done the pre-punched cards.

You could now go back and apply your own pattern to a range of hats.

Final marking up

Once all your holes are punched (and double check because it's easy to miss some) you just want to add as much information to the punchcard as possible to make it easy to follow whilst you're knitting. Things that I commonly add are stop points, colour changes, direction and name. But you can add anything that you think will be useful. As I mentioned in Chapter 3, it can also be helpful to mark up where long floats will appear that need hooking up too. Remember, though, the 5 or 7 row differential. You want to be able to see the markings on the card reader when you are knitting so they will need to be 5 or 7 rows higher than the actual row of the pattern.

Now that you have started to design and punch your own cards, you are probably eager to use them in finished projects, rather than just swatches. The first thing you can try is going back through the previous projects in this book and applying your own punchcard designs to those. Remember though that if you are using a different yarn you will need to re-calculate your gauge and amend the pattern accordingly.

PROJECT 5: CALDERISLE VEST

The following pattern is a vest that I have created with several sections designed to represent images that are personal to me, such as cups of tea and rain drops. You can practise punching cards by using this design exactly or you can experiment with adding some of your own designs instead. Have fun, play around and create something truly personal and original.

The punchcard charts for this design include sections of varying numbers of rows. One of the easiest ways to adapt this pattern to your own designs is to simply switch out one of my 18 row patterns (for example) with one of your own.

The Calderisle vest consists of sections of patterns that can be replaced with your own designs.

Or equally if you want to build up your skills over time, you could simply choose one of the pre-punched cards with your machine and use that for the entire garment instead whilst practising your construction and finishing.

Yarn
- Jamieson & Smith 100% Shetland Wool 2 ply jumper weight
- The yarn is available in 500g cones ready for machine knitting or 50g balls. If you want to use a variety of colours this gives you the option to buy a cone of your main colour and then just balls of your contrast colours.
- Approx. 250–400g total spread across six colours.
  - Col A = Shade 80 (500g)
  - Col B = Shade Fc45 (100g)
  - Col C = Shade Fc38 (50g)
  - Col D = Shade Fc34 (50g)
  - Col E = Shade 9144 (50g)
  - Col F = Shade 121 (50g)
- This will give you enough yarn for your vest as well as adequate yarn for practice swatches and tension squares, with plenty left over for other projects.

Knitting machine
Knitted on a standard gauge Knitmaster 360.

Punchcard pattern chart
The pattern is worked using the Calderisle punchcard (see Appendix) and uses six colours for the patterning.

Tension
- 28 sts and 34 rows to 10cm (4in) in Fair Isle pattern. Tension dial at T10.

Size and finished measurements

Size Chart

All measurements are taken flat. See measuring diagram for further details. The garment is knitted with approximately 8cms (3¼ in) positive ease.

The Calderisle vest.

Size		1	2	3	4	5	6	7	8
1. Chest	cm	37	42	47	52	57	62	67	70
2. Top hem	cm	35	40	45	50	55	60	65	68
3. Shoulder–shoulder (excluding ribs)	cm	26	28	30	32	34	36	38	39
4. Length from side neck (including hem)	cm	57	58	58	58	58	58	59	60
5. Armhole depth	cm	21	22	22	22	22	22	23	23
6. Neck opening (excluding ribs)	cm	14	16	18	20	22	24	26	28
7. Front neck drop	cm	15.5	16.5	16.5	16.5	16.5	16.5	17.5	17.5

Size		1	2	3	4	5	6	7	8
1. Chest	inches	14.5	16.5	18.5	20.5	22.5	24.5	26.5	27.5
2. Top hem	inches	13.75	15.75	17.75	19.75	21.75	23.75	25.75	26.75
3. Shoulder–shoulder (excluding ribs)	inches	10.25	11	11.75	12.5	13.25	14	15	15.5
4. Length from side neck (including Hem)	inches	22.5	23	23	23	23	23	23.25	23.5
5. Armhole depth	inches	8.25	8.75	8.75	8.75	8.75	8.75	9	9
6. Neck opening (excluding ribs)	inches	5.5	6.25	7	7.75	8.75	9.5	10.25	11
7. Front neck drop	inches	6	6.5	6.5	6.5	6.5	6.5	7	7

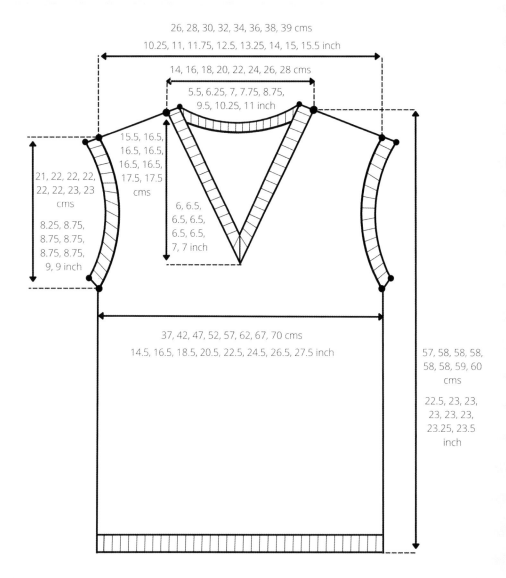

26, 28, 30, 32, 34, 36, 38, 39 cms
10.25, 11, 11.75, 12.5, 13.25, 14, 15, 15.5 inch

14, 16, 18, 20, 22, 24, 26, 28 cms
5.5, 6.25, 7, 7.75, 8.75,
9.5, 10.25, 11 inch

15.5, 16.5,
16.5, 16.5,
16.5, 16.5,
17.5, 17.5
cms

21, 22, 22, 22,
22, 22, 23, 23
cms

8.25, 8.75,
8.75, 8.75,
8.75, 8.75,
9, 9 inch

6, 6.5,
6.5, 6.5,
6.5, 6.5,
7, 7 inch

37, 42, 47, 52, 57, 62, 67, 70 cms
14.5, 16.5, 18.5, 20.5, 22.5, 24.5, 26.5, 27.5 inch

57, 58, 58, 58,
58, 58, 59, 60
cms

22.5, 23, 23,
23, 23, 23,
23.25, 23.5
inch

Colour charts

See Appendix at the back of the book.

Pattern instructions

The pattern below is written to include a rib hem,
armholes and neckline. If you do not have a ribber
attachment, then you can use a mock rib on your
main bed instead.

Vest back

Instruction	Tension	Needles in work	Row count
RC to 000. Cast on 106 (120, 134, 148, 162, 176, 190, 198) sts in MC A in 2x2 rib setup	T0	106 (120, 134, 148, 162, 176, 190, 198)	0
K16R of 2x2 rib in MC A	T6		16
Trfr sts to MB. RC to 000	T10		0
Insert punchcard into machine and lock in start position			
K2R in MC A	T10	106 (120, 134, 148, 162, 176, 190, 198)	2
Switch Fair Isle knitting on (see Chapter 1 if you need a reminder how to do this)			
K100R of Fair Isle changing colours as per the colour chart. Continue to follow the colour charts for the remainder of the knitting.	T10	106 (120, 134, 148, 162, 176, 190, 198)	102
Armhole shaping			
CO 2 (2, 3, 3, 4, 5, 6, 6) sts at beg of nxt 8R	T10	90 (104, 110, 124, 130, 136, 142, 150)	110
Dec 1st f/f each side at beg of nxt and every foll alt row x 9 (12, 13, 17, 17, 18, 18, 20) times	T10	72 (80, 84, 90, 96, 100, 106, 110)	128 (134, 136, 144, 144, 146, 146, 150)
K42 (40, 38, 30, 30, 28, 32, 32) R. COR.	T10	72 (80, 84, 90, 96, 100, 106, 110)	170 (174, 174, 174, 174, 174, 178, 182)
Shoulder shaping			
*Switch Carr to Hold. Push 3 sts at LHS to Hold & K1R. W&T. COL.	T10	69 (77, 81, 87, 93, 97, 103, 107)	171 (175, 175, 175, 175, 175, 179, 183)
Push 3 sts at RHS to Hold & K1R. W&T. COR.*	T10	66 (74, 78, 84, 90, 94, 100, 104)	172 (176, 176, 176, 176, 176, 180, 184)
Rep * to * twice more	T10	54 (62, 66, 72, 78, 82, 88, 92)	176 (180, 180, 180, 180, 180, 184, 188)
Neck shaping RHS			
Put ctr 40 (44, 50, 56, 62, 68, 74, 80) sts into Hold position.			
Put rem 7 (9, 8, 8, 8, 7, 7, 6) sts on LHS into Hold position. COR.		7 (9, 8, 8, 8, 7, 7, 6) on RHS	
NOTE: Make a note of your punchcard row at this point.			
K1R. Push 2 ndls to Hold at end of nxt row. W&T. K1R Rep from * to * twice more.	T10	1 (3, 2, 2, 2, 1, 1, 0)	182 (186, 186, 186, 186, 186, 190, 194)
Put 16 (18, 17, 17, 17, 16, 16, 15) ndls on RHS back into work and K2R	T10	16 (18, 17, 17, 17, 16, 16, 15)	184 (188, 188, 188, 188, 188, 192, 196)
CO 16 (18, 17, 17, 17, 16, 16, 15) sts on RHS onto WY		0	
Neck shaping LHS			
COR. You should now have 56 (62, 67, 74, 79, 84, 90, 95) sts on your ndls. Working from RHS keep the nxt 40 (44, 50, 56, 62, 68, 74, 80) ndls in Hold position. Push the nxt 7 (9, 8, 8, 8, 7, 7, 6) back into working position. This will leave a further 9 ndls in Hold on the LHS. Keep Carr set to Hold.	T10	7 (9, 8, 8, 8, 7, 7, 6)	
Turn punchcard back to same point as start of neck shaping on RHS. Pick up Fair Isle patterning on the needles. Reset RC. Turn Fair Isle on.			176 (180, 180, 180, 180, 180, 184, 188)
Push 2 ndls to Hold at end of nxt row. K1R. W&T. K1R. Rep from * to * twice more.	T10	1 (3, 2, 2, 2, 1, 1, 0)	182 (186, 186, 186, 186, 186, 190, 194)
Put 16 (18, 17, 17, 17, 16, 16, 15) ndls on LHS back into work and K2R	T10	16 (18, 17, 17, 17, 16, 16, 15)	184 (188, 188, 188, 188, 188, 192, 196)
CO 16 (18, 17, 17, 17, 16, 16, 15) sts on LHS onto WY			
Put rem 40 (44, 50, 56, 62, 68, 74, 80) ndls back into work and K2R	T10	40 (44, 50, 56, 62, 68, 74, 80)	
CO 40 (44, 50, 56, 62, 68, 74, 80) sts onto WY			

Vest front

Instruction	Tension	Needles in work	Row count
Knit exactly as Back as far as Armhole shaping		106 (120, 134, 148, 162, 176, 190, 198)	102
Armhole shaping			
CO 2 (2, 3, 3, 4, 5, 6, 6) sts at beg of nxt 8R	T10	90 (104, 110, 124, 130, 136, 142, 150)	110
Dec 1st f/f each side at beg of nxt and every foll alt row x 9 times. COR.	T10	72 (86, 92, 106, 112, 118, 124, 132)	128
Divide for V neck RHS			
Push 36 (43, 46, 53, 56, 59, 62, 66) ndls on LHS into Hold position. Set Carr to Hold.		36 (43, 46, 53, 56, 59, 62, 66)	128
NOTE: Make a note of your punchcard row at this point.			
Dec 1st f/f each side at beg of nxt and every foll alt row 0 (3, 4, 8, 8, 9, 9, 11) times.	T10	36 (37, 38, 37, 40, 41, 44, 44)	128 (134, 136, 144, 144, 146, 146, 150)
Dec 1st f/f at neck edge only on nxt and every fall alt row 20 (13, 13, 4, 7, 3, 4, 3) times.	T10	16 (24, 25, 33, 33, 38, 40, 41)	168 (160, 162, 152, 158, 152, 154, 156)
Dec 1st f/f at neck edge only on every row 0 (6, 8, 16, 16, 22, 24, 26) times.	T10	16 (18, 17, 17, 17, 16, 16, 15)	168 (166, 170, 168, 174, 174, 178, 182)
K2 (8, 4, 6, 0, 0, 0, 0) R. COR.	T10	16 (18, 17, 17, 17, 16, 16, 15)	170 (174, 174, 174, 174, 174, 178, 182)
Shoulder shaping RHS			
K1R. Push 3 sts at RHS to Hold & K1R. W&T. Rep twice more. COR.	T10	7 (9, 8, 8, 8, 7, 7, 6)	176 (180, 180, 180, 180, 180, 184, 188)
K1R. Push 2 ndls to Hold at RHS. W&T. K1R Rep from * to * twice more.	T10	1 (3, 2, 2, 2, 1, 1, 0)	182 (186, 186, 186, 186, 186, 190, 194)
Put 16 (18, 17, 17, 17, 16, 16, 15) ndls on RHS back into work and K2R	T10	16 (18, 17, 17, 17, 16, 16, 15)	184 (188, 188, 188, 188, 188, 192, 196)
CO 16 (18, 17, 17, 17, 16, 16, 15) sts on RHS onto WY		0	
Knit V neck LHS			
Turn punchcard back to same point as start of v-neck shaping on RHS. Pick up Fair Isle patterning on the needles. Reset RC. Turn Fair Isle on.			128
Put 36 (43, 46, 53, 56, 59, 62, 66) ndls on LHS back into work. Cancel Hold on Carr. COR.		36 (43, 46, 53, 56, 59, 62, 66)	128
Dec 1st f/f each side at beg of nxt and every foll alt row 0 (3, 4, 8, 8, 9, 9, 11) times.	T10	36 (37, 38, 37, 40, 41, 44, 44)	128 (134, 136, 144, 144, 146, 146, 150)
Dec 1st f/f at neck edge only on nxt and every fall alt row 20 (13, 13, 4, 7, 3, 4, 3) times.	T10	16 (24, 25, 33, 33, 38, 40, 41)	168 (160, 162, 152, 158, 152, 154, 156)
Dec 1st f/f at neck edge only on every row 0 (6, 8, 16, 16, 22, 24, 26) times.	T10	16 (18, 17, 17, 17, 16, 16, 15)	168 (166, 170, 168, 174, 174, 178, 182)
K2 (8, 4, 6, 0, 0, 0, 0) R. COR.	T10	16 (18, 17, 17, 17, 16, 16, 15)	170 (174, 174, 174, 174, 174, 178, 182)
Shoulder shaping LHS			
Set Carr to Hold. *Push 3 sts at LHS to Hold & K1R. W&T. K1R.* Rep twice more. COR.	T10	7 (9, 8, 8, 8, 7, 7, 6)	176 (180, 180, 180, 180, 180, 184, 188)
Push 2 ndls at LHS to Hold & K1R. W&T. K1R Rep from * to * twice more.	T10	1 (3, 2, 2, 2, 1, 1, 0)	182 (186, 186, 186, 186, 186, 190, 194)
Put 16 (18, 17, 17, 17, 16, 16, 15) ndls on LHS back into work and K2R	T10	16 (18, 17, 17, 17, 16, 16, 15)	184 (188, 188, 188, 188, 188, 192, 196)
CO 16 (18, 17, 17, 17, 16, 16, 15) sts on RHS onto WY		0	

Making up – part 1

See Chapter 3 for details on how to block your knitting. Pin out your front and back pieces to the measurements given at the start of the pattern. Once dry, continue with pattern below.

Neck and armhole trims

Instruction	Tension	Needles in work	Row count
Neckband			
Join one of the shoulder seams by pulling the stitches from the Front piece through the Back piece.			
Starting at the bottom of the V neck on the Front piece pick up 80 (84, 88, 92, 92, 96, 104, 108) sts from the front neck and half of the back neck edge with WS facing you.		80 (84, 88, 92, 92, 96, 104, 108)	0
RC to 000. K1R	T9		1
Trfr sts to 2x2 rib setup & insert rib comb and weights.		80 (84, 88, 92, 92, 96, 104, 108)	
K8R starting at T6 and dec one point every 2R.	T6/ T5.2/T5.1/T5	80 (84, 88, 92, 92, 96, 104, 108)	9
CO. Join the other shoulder seam and rep on other side.			
Use mattress stitch to join your neck trims at CB and CF. At CF mitre your edge.			
Armholes			
Starting with the shoulder seam in the C of your bed, pick up 68 (72, 76, 76, 80, 80, 88, 88) sts each side from the armhole edge.		68 (72, 76, 76, 80, 80, 88, 88)	
RC to 000. K1R	T9		1
Trfr sts to 2x2 rib setup & insert rib comb and weights.		68 (72, 76, 76, 80, 80, 88, 88)	
K8R starting at T6 and dec one point every 2R.	T6/ T5.2/T5.1/T5	68 (72, 76, 76, 80, 80, 88, 88)	9
CO.			

Making up – part 2

Finish the side seams of your vest, including the armhole trim and the hem in your preferred method.

    Wash and steam your vest one final time.

You can knit my version of the Calderisle vest or create your own using punchcards of your choice.

CHAPTER 6

TAKING FAIR ISLE FURTHER

The previous five chapters should have whetted your appetite for the potential of Fair Isle knitting on your machine. In this final chapter, we will explore the opportunities for taking this technique even further to create truly unique knitwear. You should be feeling much more confident with the basic principles of Fair Isle and now you can begin to have much more fun by playing around, experimenting, and doing your own thing.

PARTIAL KNITTING

Although I introduced you to partial knitting in Chapter 4, that was covering the conventional use of partial knitting for working on sections of a garment such as either side of a neckline. That application was still using Fair Isle over the entire shoulder pieces. In the same chapter, we also covered how you could use motif knitting to include vertical panels of pattern rather than covering the full width of the knitting. But you can extend the principle further by using partial knitting to combine Fair Isle and shaping at the same time, wherever you want it, by putting needles in and out of work by design.

With clever planning, Fair Isle can be added wherever you want it.

Knitting triangles and diagonals

Sometimes it can be difficult to visualize how this technique will work but it follows the same basic principle that the patterning will only happen on needles that are in work and anything in D or E will just hold the stitches. So you can cast on in one colour and knit a few rows before switching. Then switch to Hold position and move all the needles out all the way to D or E except the two nearest to the carriage. Start Fair Isle knitting and then every two rows, move the next two needles back into B position with your transfer tool. If you continue like this all the way across the bed until all needles are back in position, you will have created a triangle of Fair Isle. If you then switch Fair Isle off and start with the carriage on the opposite side, repeat the same instructions with one colour knitting and you will now have a corresponding triangle in single colour stocking stitch. You could carry on like this for several repeats and see what happens. Then you could try smaller triangles or different degrees of diagonal. You should begin to see that your options are almost endless.

Moving pairs of needles back into work every two rows to create triangles of Fair Isle.

Using partial knitting you can create diagonal edges to patterning very easily.

Frills and godets

Partial knitting can also be used to good effect to create ruffles and frills. By adding volume into certain sections of your knitting only those areas will kick out. If you switch on Fair Isle at the same time as you are knitting these fuller sections and switch it off and revert to single colour knitting for the other sections you will create godet panels of patterning.

HAND MANIPULATION

As with partial knitting, once you are confident with Fair Isle you can begin to combine it with other techniques as well. Because Fair Isle always needs to be operated by your punchcard, it isn't possible to combine it with other punchcard functions such as tuck or slip. But you can use hand manipulation in combination with your Fair Isle patterning to add more interest.

Tuck stitch

Just because you can't use a punchcard for tuck stitch, it doesn't mean you can't combine it with Fair Isle as well. Tuck is a great stitch for adding texture and dimension to your knitting. When combined with a flat Fair Isle pattern, this can create a really interesting juxtaposition. To replicate tuck stitch manually all you need to do is push a needle that you want to tuck out to D or E position. Switch your machine to hold position and continue to knit in Fair Isle. Once you have knitted your desired number of tuck rows (normally four or less) you can cancel Hold and use your transfer tool to hook the original stitch and the floats back onto the needle. Continue knitting and all the floats will be knitted and tucked into the stitch on the next row.

Remember, though, that the tucks are most effective on the reverse of the fabric and a lot of punchcard patterns are designed with the front of the fabric in mind so you would need to be careful

Another fun use of partial knitting with Fair Isle can result in sections or godets of pattern that add shaping as well.

selecting a pattern that is still distinctive on the reverse or design a pattern specifically.

Cable and pointelle

The most effective use of these combinations will probably require a little planning in order to give the maximum impact but you could start by playing around and experimenting. Perhaps pop in a Fair Isle card you already have and as you are knitting, choose certain needles to add cables to. Cables could start and finish in certain coloured sections and not in others. Again, your options will be numerous.

Alternatively you could start by moving certain single needles out of work entirely for a whole section to create ladders. This will be particularly effective on patterns that have a strong vertical line to the pattern. Or you could move stitches onto neighbouring needles but leave the empty needle in work to create eyelets in certain sections.

Once you have begun to get a feel for what works and doesn't with a particular pattern you could begin to design the layout more consciously and chart out a design marking on exactly where the two colours appear and where you will add cables and pointelle.

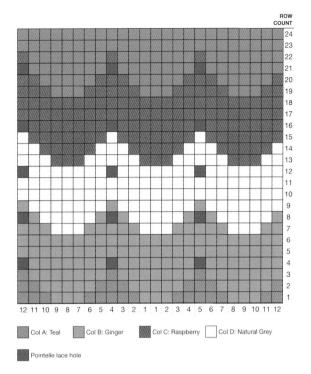

	ROW COUNT
	24
	23
	22
	21
	20
	19
	18
	17
	16
	15
	14
	13
	12
	11
	10
	9
	8
	7
	6
	5
	4
	3
	2
	1

12 11 10 9 8 7 6 5 4 3 2 1 1 2 3 4 5 6 7 8 9 10 11 12

Col A: Teal   Col B: Ginger   Col C: Raspberry   Col D: Natural Grey

Pointelle lace hole

Adding pointelle lace holes intentionally on this design will add a nice lacey effect and make the pattern a great design for summer garments.

Expanding patterns past the 24-stitch repeat

This technique is also a good option for knitters who have a machine with no punchcard facility as it is effectively hand patterning your Fair Isle. Previously in the book I have discussed the restrictions imposed by having to use the 24-stitch repeat for any knitting. But this is actually only a half truth. There is absolutely nothing to stop you knitting a single motif of your pattern in the centre of your garment and then hand manipulating the stitches for two-colour knitting either side of it.

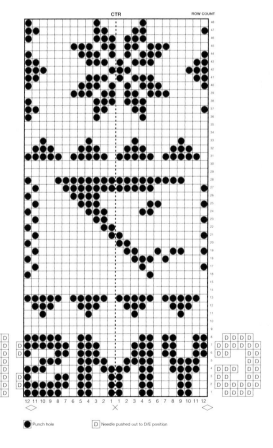

This chart contains a repeating Fair Isle pattern across the centre 24 stitches. For the first 8 rows that contain lettering, the words have been created with hand manipulation either side of a single motif before switching back to all-over Fair Isle from Row 9 onwards.

● Punch hole   D Needle pushed out to D/E position

Hand manipulated Fair Isle

Now that you fully understand how the needles operate for Fair Isle knitting you should be able to see how you would be able to create a design manually. Any needles that you push out to C or D/E position will always knit the contrast colour whilst any needles in B will always knit the main colour. If you want to experiment quickly, to try this out, set everything up for Fair Isle but don't use a punchcard. Instead use just two colours and randomly switch needles between B and D/E and see how the machine responds.

This is what the punchcard pattern looks like when it's knitted.

FAIR ISLE YOKES AND SHAPING

There is one particular style of garment that is synonymous with Fair Isle knitting and that is the patterned yoke jumper which has a single colour body and sleeves, topped with a colourful patterned yoke. They are a popular style in both hand and machine knitting and very often combine both techniques in the same garment. This might even be one of the next garments you are planning on knitting now that you have mastered Fair Isle punchcards. There are a few additional things that you need to consider so that your yoke patterning works effectively.

Patterned Fair Isle yokes require a little additional planning to make them really effective.

A Fair Isle yoke is actually a clever piece of design. It is nothing more than three or four rectangles of Fair Isle with decreases between each rectangle that help to pull the pattern in and create a semi-circular shape.

There can be variations on the raglan jumper design and it can be designed to be knitted from the bottom up or the top down, but the principles for creating the yoke remain the same.

If you are planning to design your own patterned yoke you will need to do some planning with the pattern that you intend to use so that you can design

The yoke is shaped by decreasing between each of the levels of patterning.

where and how often your decreases will appear. If you want to make it easier for yourself, you can add 2 rows of plain knitting at the start of each section and complete the decreases in the plain rows. This way you don't have to worry about them affecting the pattern layout. If you don't have plain rows and want to decrease on a patterned row you will need to make sure that you can accommodate the decreases without affecting the balance of the pattern.

If you plan your patterning well your decreases should be invisible and your patterning should flow nicely from bottom to top.

A collection of successful Fair Isle knitting.

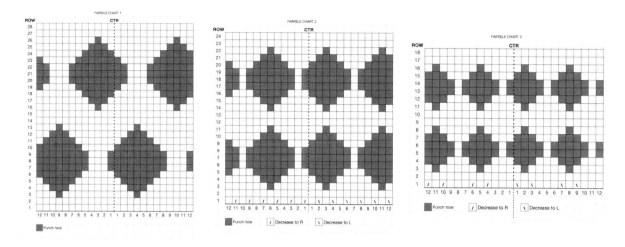

These three Fair Isle charts have a 12-, 8- and 6-stitch repeat which will all fit onto a 12- or 24-stitch punchcard so will work well. The charts also show where you would decrease on the plain rows to get even shaping.

If you want to experiment and begin to understand how this will work you can use the charts pictured and knit a mini-yoke in the following way:

1. Cast on 50 stitches in main colour and knit 10 rows.
2. Switch to Chart 1 pattern and knit two colour Fair Isle to row 28 (the first 2 rows will be main colour only).
3. Remove the yoke on waste yarn.
4. Pick up the knitting back onto the machine with the wrong side facing you and place 2 stitches on every needle marked as a decrease on the chart. You should now have 26 stitches remaining.
5. Switch to Chart 2 pattern and knit two colour Fair Isle to row 24 (again, Rows 1 and 2 are main colour only).
6. Remove the yoke on waste yarn.
7. Pick up the knitting back onto the machine with the wrong side facing you and place 2 stitches on every needle marked as a decrease on the chart. You should now have 18 stitches remaining.
8. Switch to Chart 3 pattern and knit two colour Fair Isle to row 18 (again, Rows 1 and 2 are main colour only).
9. You can now cast off or remove onto waste yarn.

If you examine your sample you should have a wedge-shaped piece of knitting with the patterning decreasing towards the top.

PLAYING AROUND AND EXPERIMENTING

Now that we are coming to the end of this book, I hope that you feel much more knowledgeable about Fair Isle machine knitting and inspired enough to go it alone. This book has really only scratched the surface when it comes to the possibilities of Fair Isle knitting and this is one of the reasons I love it so much. You should now feel confident enough to play around and experiment to your heart's content and create designs that are truly original to you.

PUNCHCARDS AND COLOUR CHARTS FOR PROJECTS

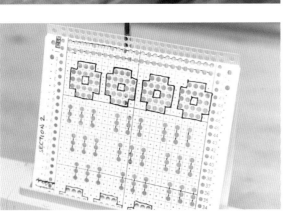

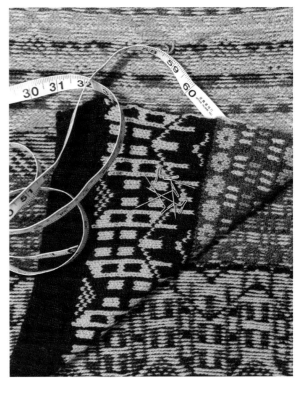

PROJECT 2: SIMPLE FAIR ISLE COWL AND WRIST WARMERS IN MULTIPLE COLOURS

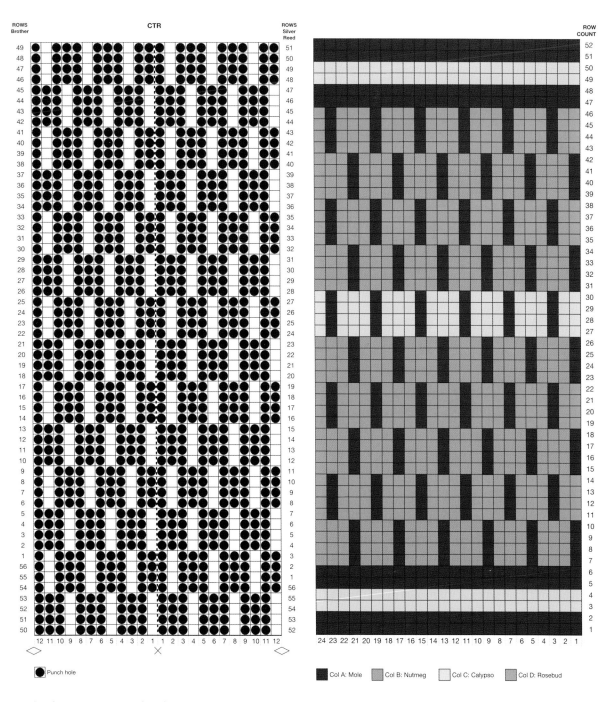

Cowl and wrist warmers punchcard.

Wrist warmer colour chart.

Col A: Mole   Col B: Nutmeg   Col C: Calypso   Col D: Rosebud

● Punch hole

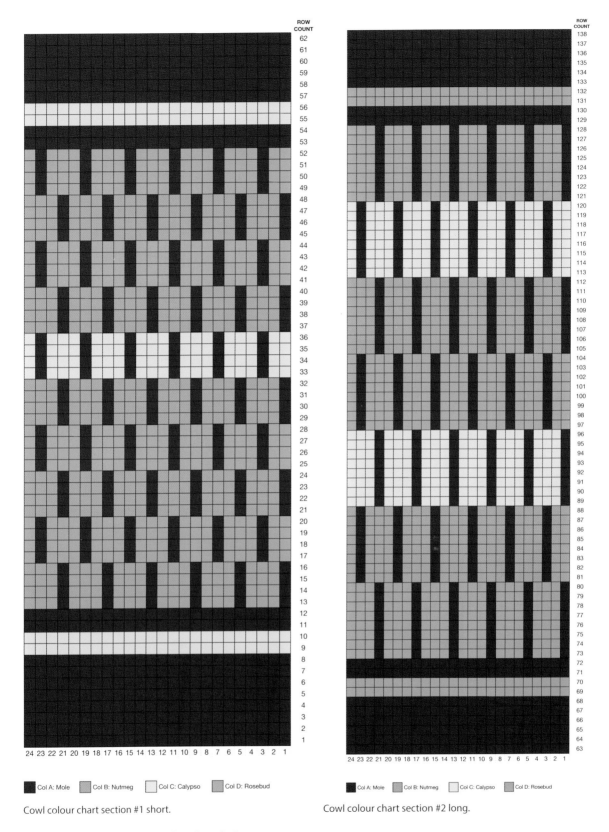

Cowl colour chart section #1 short.

Cowl colour chart section #2 long.

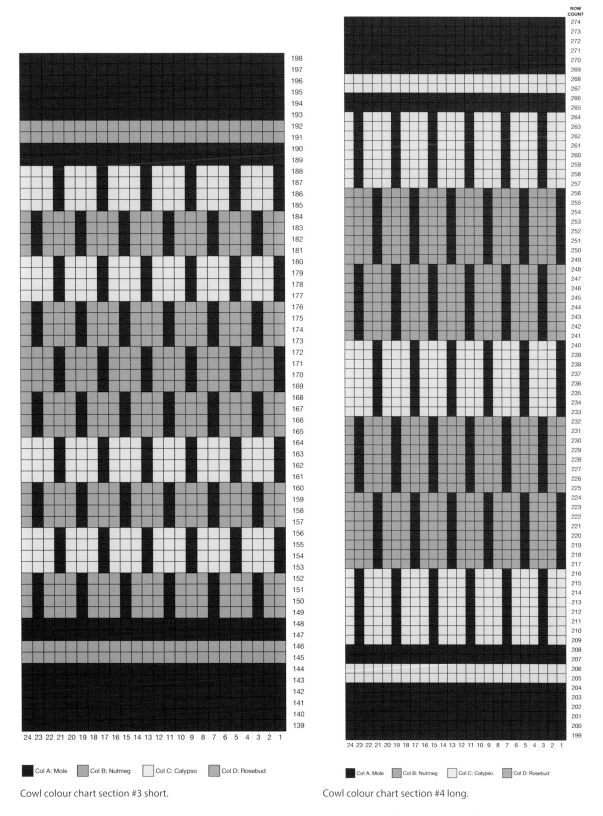

Cowl colour chart section #3 short.

Cowl colour chart section #4 long.

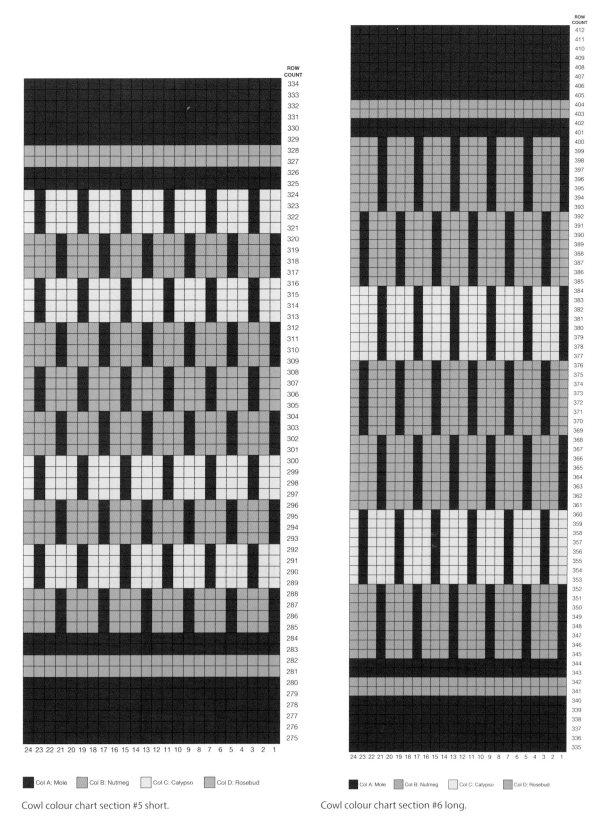

Cowl colour chart section #5 short.

Cowl colour chart section #6 long.

PROJECT 3: NORTHERN WAVES PATTERNED CUSHION COVER

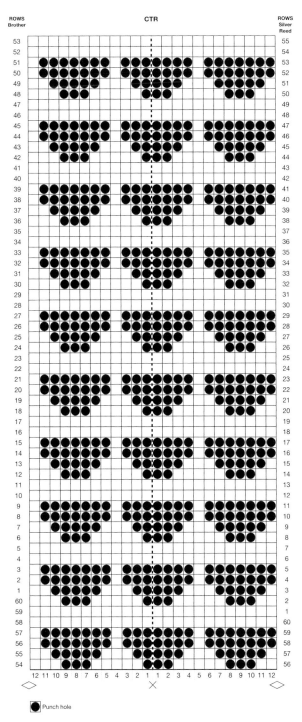

Punch hole

Northern Waves cushion punchcard.

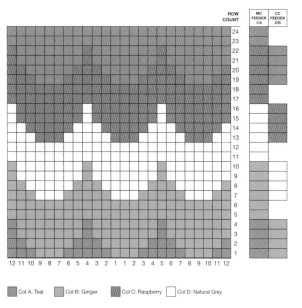

Col A: Teal Col B: Ginger Col C: Raspberry Col D: Natural Grey

Northern Waves cushion colour chart.

PROJECT 4: NORTH UIST POM-POM HAT

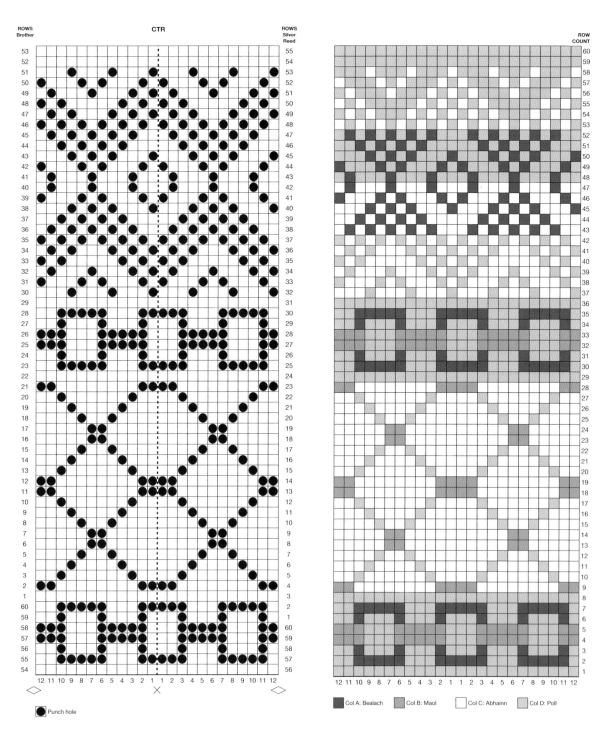

Uist hat punchcard.

Uist hat colour chart.

PROJECT 5: CALDERISLE VEST

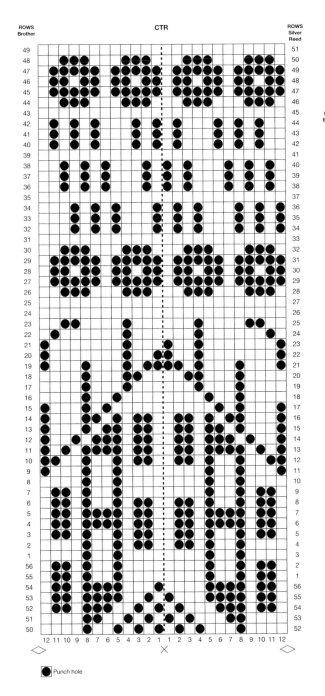

Calderisle vest punchcard sections 1 and 2.

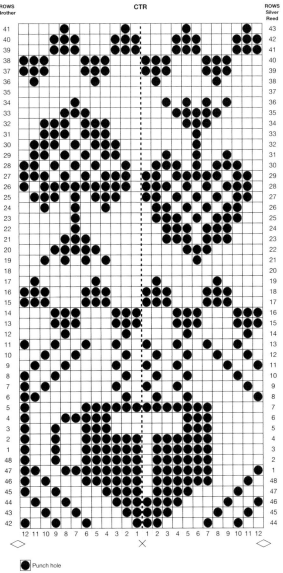

Calderisle vest punchcard sections 3–6.

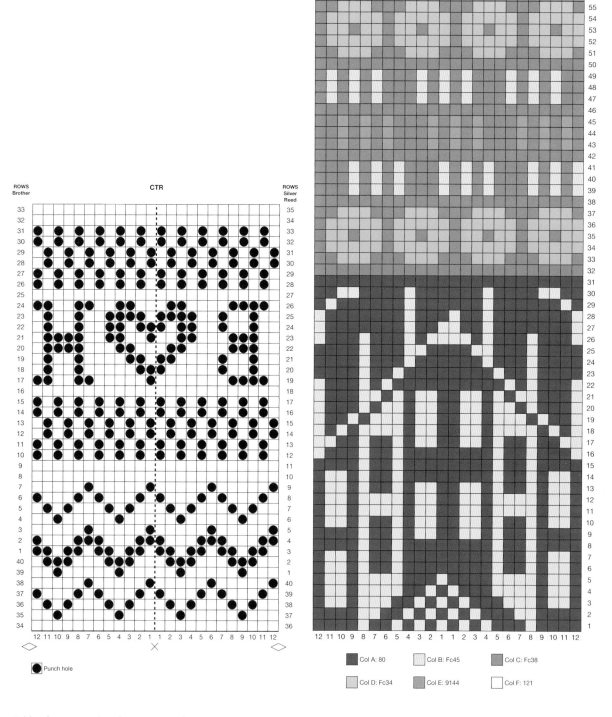

Calderisle vest punchcard sections 7 and 8.

Calderisle vest colour chart sections 1 and 2 (rows 1–56).

Col A: 80 Col B: Fc45 Col C: Fc38

Col D: Fc34 Col E: 9144 Col F: 121

Calderisle vest colour chart sections 3–6 (rows 57–104).

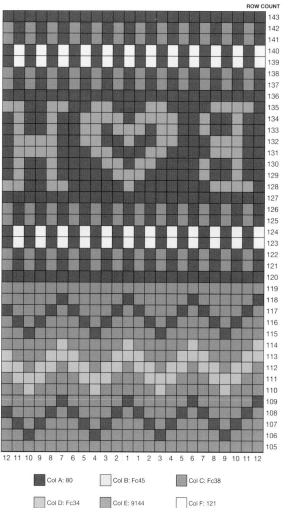

Col A: 80 Col B: Fc45 Col C: Fc38

Col D: Fc34 Col E: 9144 Col F: 121

Calderisle vest colour chart sections 3–6 (rows 105–143).

Col A: 80   Col B: Fc45   Col C: Fc38

Col D: Fc34   Col E: 9144   Col F: 121

Calderisle vest colour chart sections 1 and 2 (rows 144–200).

ABBREVIATIONS

- alt = alternate
- betw = between
- C = centre
- carr = carriage
- CB = centre back
- CF = centre front
- CO = cast off
- COL = carriage on left
- COR = carriage on right
- dec = decrease
- f/f = fully fashioned
- foll = following
- inc = increase
- K = knit
- LHS = left hand side
- LN = left needle
- MB = main bed

- MC = main colour
- MT = main tension (the chosen tension for the body of your garment)
- Ndl/s = needle/s
- nxt = next
- R = row/s
- RB = ribber bed
- RC = row count
- Rem = remaining
- Rep = repeat
- RHS = right hand side
- RN = right needle
- Sts = stitch/es
- T = tension
- Trfr = transfer
- W&T = wrap and turn
- WY = waste yarn

BIBLIOGRAPHY

LIST OF SUPPLIERS

Allen, J., *Fabulous Fair Isle*. Lochar Publishing, 1991.

Bauer, A., *Alterknit Rebellion*. David and Charles Ltd, 2019.

Devaney, B., *The Harmony Guide to Colourful Machine Knitting*. Lyric Books Ltd, 1989.

Don, S., *Fair Isle Knitting*. Mills & Boon, 1979.

Haffenden, V., *Translating Between Hand and Machine Knitting*. Crowood Press, 2018.

Lee, R., *Patterning on the Knitting Machine*. Batsford, 1989.

Phillips, W., *Folk & Fair Isle: Over 100 Designs*. Middletons of Ambleside, 1987.

Russel, M., *Fair Isle Knitting: A Practical & Inspirational Guide*. Search Press Limited, 2019.

Sharp, H., *Linking Knitwear*. Helen Sharp, 2019.

Smith, M. and Twatt, M., *A Shetland Pattern Book*. The Shetland Times Ltd,1979.

Spurling, F., *Designing Knitted Textiles*. Laurence King Publishing, 2021.

Starmore, A., *Alice Starmore's Book of Fair Isle Knitting*. Dover Publications, 1988.

KNITTING MACHINES – SUPPLIERS AND SPARE PARTS

Andee Knits
Machines, repairs and parts
www.machine-knitting.co.uk

Hague Direct
Linkers and parts
www.haguedirect.co.uk

Spartan Knitting Machine Parts
Spare parts and accessories
www.ebay.com/str/tprknittingmachineparts

To download instruction manuals for your machine:
www.mkmanuals.com

YARNS

United Kingdom

Fairfield Yarns
www.fairfieldyarns.co.uk

J.C. Rennie
www.knitrennie.com

FURTHER RESOURCES

Jamieson & Smith
www.shetlandwoolbrokers.co.uk

Jamiesons of Shetland
www.jamiesonsofshetland.co.uk

Northern Yarn
www.northernyarn.co.uk

Uist Wool
www.uistwool.com

Uppingham Yarns
www.wools.co.uk

Wool Circle
www.woolcircle.uk

Woolyknit
www.woolyknit.com

North America

Altis Studio
www.altisstudio.com

Adapting patterns for different gauges and tension
https://www.mkc.
community/free-mini-
workshops/tensions

Blocking your knitwear
https://www.mkc.
community/free-mini-
workshops/block-knitwear

Knitting graph paper
www.theknittingsite.com/
knitting-graph-paper
www.sweaterscapes.com/land-
chart-paper.htm

Linking
I would highly recommend the book *Linking Knitwear* by Helen Sharp for a detailed insight into uses for your linker.

Pulling back rows in machine knitting
'Ripping rows' at https://youtu.
be/x-7khPMhmKk

Software for knitting pattern designing
www.envisioknit.com

Software for charting your own patterns
www.stitchfiddle.com

Tension squares
https://www.mkc.
community/free-mini-
workshops/tensions

ACKNOWLEDGEMENTS

All photographs in this book are courtesy of Joanne Crawford except for the following: Photo of Marie Bruhat is courtesy of Tessa Bunney; photos of work by artists Lisa Anne Auerbach, Kandy Diamond and Sophie Ochera are artists' own.

I am extremely grateful to The Crowood Press who have shown the belief in the craft of machine knitting and whose support has been invaluable. Their commitment to creating a modern library of resource tools for machine knitters will help the craft to thrive.

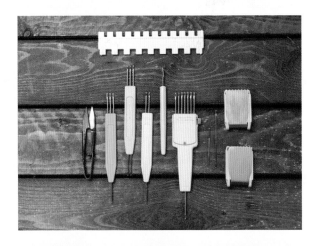

I would also like to thank Kate at Northern Yarn, Uist Wools, J.C. Rennie, and Jamieson & Smith for their generous yarn support which allowed me to design the new patterns in this book with some of the nicest yarns available.

I wouldn't be in a position to write a book like this without all the help and support I have received over the course of my machine knitting journey. From the staff and technicians at UCLan, where I trained, and especially Leanne who allowed me to sleep on her floor when taking breaks from the knitting machine in our final year at university, to Judi and Irene who were wonderful mentors during my time at Coast. Also, June at Halifax Machine Knitting Club who helped me so much when my business was in its infancy. And not forgetting all the wonderful members of the Machine Knit Community who motivate and inspire me every day, including Katie my able assistant and third arm at the knitting machine.

Finally, I have a deep gratitude for my friend Marie Bruhat who has introduced me to Fair Isle itself and deepened my love and understanding of both the island and the knitwear that originates from there.